REACTIONARY ESSAYS ON
POETRY AND IDEAS

REACTIONARY ESSAYS ON POETRY AND IDEAS

By

ALLEN TATE

Teaching the cause why all those flames that rise
From forms external can no longer last.
—The Ocean to Cynthia.

CHARLES SCRIBNER'S SONS · NEW YORK
CHARLES SCRIBNER'S SONS · LTD · LONDON
1936

To J. C. R.

FOR SUFFICIENT REASON

ACKNOWLEDGEMENTS

The essay on the late Hart Crane is made up of three papers, one written when *The Bridge* appeared in 1930, the two others after his death two years later. *Religion and the Old South* is a lengthened version of my contribution to *I'll Take My Stand* (Harper's, 1930), which is out of print. *Humanism and Naturalism* was published as *The Fallacy of Humanism* in Mr. C. Hartley Grattan's symposium *The Critique of Humanism* (Brewer and Warren, 1930). I am grateful to the editors of magazines in which parts of this book first appeared: *The New Republic, The Symposium, The Nation, The Virginia Quarterly Review, The Hound and Horn, The Criterion, Poetry: A Magazine of Verse,* and *The Southern Review*.

For critical reading of the manuscript I am indebted to Mr. Stark Young and to my colleagues, Professors A. T. Johnson, Samuel H. Monk, and W. T. Jones.

PREFACE

MODERN poets are having trouble with form, and must use "ideas" in a new fashion that seems wilfully obscure to all readers but the most devoted. The public waits to be convinced that the poets behave as they do because they cannot help it. That is one of the uses of criticism at the present time.

How have poets used ideas in the past? How are they using them today? How shall we explain the difference between the poet's situation in the past and his present situation? Or, if explanation is beyond us, as it probably is, what terms shall we call in merely to record the changes that have brought about the modern situation? It is, I think, our task to find out what the poets have done, not what they ought to have done, and to guess what it was possible for them to do in their times. But even the right guess would be a truism: what a poet wrote was alone possible for him to write. It is nevertheless a duty of the modern critic to notice the implication of the impossible, if only to warn the reader of modern verse, who is exasperated, that poets cannot write now like poets in 1579.

Poetry in some sense has a great deal to do with our experience. Historians exhibit its general features as evidence to support still more general theories of history and society. But modern literary critics are reversing the procedure of the historian. They are using social theories to prove something about poetry. It is a heresy that has, of course, reared its head before, yet never more formidably than now. We are trying to make a fine art respectable by showing that after all it is only a branch of politics: we are justifying poetry by "proving" that it is something else, just as, I believe, we have justified religion with the discovery that it is science.

Now to order our political interests is to practise one of the greater arts. Both politics and the arts must derive their power from a common center of energy. It is not certain that the old theory of art for art's sake is more absurd than its perfect analogy—politics for politics' sake, which as an abstraction becomes Economics that we pursue as truth-in-itself. It is agreed that our political confusion is alarming. It is not agreed that it will continue to be alarming until we are able to see our belief in the absolute of a scientific society as at least a phase, if not profoundly the cause, of our confusion. Both politics and poetry, having ceased to be arts, are cut off from their common center of energy. They try to nourish each other. It is a diminishing diet. The neo-communists are not likely to grow fatter on it than their capitalist brethren by giving it a new name. For a political poetry, or a poetical politics, of whatever denomination is a society of two members living on each other's washing. They devour each other in the end. It is the heresy of spiritual cannibalism.

This heresy is a legitimate field of modern criticism, but because it denies the traditional procedure of poets and is hence negative, it will concern the poet only in his faculty of critic, not in his job as craftsman. The poet's special question is: How shall the work be done? Why it was done and why the work is what it is, questions of first interest to readers of poetry, are of little interest to poets who are able to remain artists in a difficult age.

For poetry does not explain our experience. If we begin by thinking that it ought to "explain" the human predicament, we shall quickly see that it does not, and we shall end up thinking that therefore it has no meaning at all. That is what Mr. I. A. Richards' theory comes to at last, and it is the first assumption of criticism today. But poetry is at once more modest and, in the great poets, more profound. It is the art of apprehending and concentrating our experience in the mysterious limitations of form.

Philosophy even in the strict sense may be the material of poetry, but poets are not chiefly philosophers. A poet whose main passion is to get his doctrine—or his personality or his local color—into his poems is trying to justify a medium in which he lacks confidence. There is a division of purpose, and the arrogance of facile "solutions" that thinks it can get along without experience. The poet had better write his poetry first; examine it; then decide what he thinks. The poetry may not reveal all that he thinks; it will reveal all he thinks that is any good—for poetry. Poetry is one test of ideas; it is ideas tested by experience, by the act of direct apprehension.

There are all kinds of poetry readers. The innocent reader and the reader till lately called the moralist, who is now the social reader, are different from the critical reader, and they are both incurably intellectual. Their heads buzz with generalizations that they expect the poet to confirm —so that they will not have to notice the poetry. This is a service that the modern poet, no less amiable than his forbears, is not ready to perform: there is no large scheme of imaginative reference in which he has confidence. He must, in short, attach some irony to his use of "ideas," which tend to wither; he may look for a new growth but with the reservation that it too may be subject to the natural decay.

The innocent reader lives in the past; he likes to see in poetry, if not the conscious ideas, then the sensibility of a previous age. Our future sensibility the social reader, wise as he is, has no way of predicting, because he ignores the one source of that kind of prophecy—the present—grasped in terms, not of abstractions, but of experience; so he demands that poets shall set forth the ideas that he, in his facility, has decided that the future will live by. The poet—and it is he who is the critical reader—is aware of the present, any present, now or past or future. For by experiencing the past along with the present he makes present the past, and masters it; and he alone is at the center of the experience out of which the future must come. The social reader ought to remember that the specialist worries the major works of Spenser as a hungry dog his bone, but that the Divine Comedy has been at the center of our minds for six hundred years. The greater poets give us knowledge, not of the new programs, but of ourselves.

A. T.

Southwestern
Memphis
February 16, 1936

CONTENTS

ESSAYS

FOUR AMERICAN POETS

I. Emily Dickinson

GREAT poetry needs no special features of difficulty to make it mysterious. When it has them, the reputation of the poet is likely to remain ambiguous. This is still true of Donne, and it is true of Emily Dickinson, whose verse appeared in an age unfavorable to the exercise of intelligence in poetry. Her poetry is not like any other poetry of her time; it is not like any of the innumerable kinds of verse written today. In still another respect it is far removed from us. It is a poetry of ideas, and it demands of the reader a point of view—not an opinion of the New Deal or of the League of Nations, but an ingrained philosophy that is fundamental, a kind of settled attitude that is almost extinct in this eclectic age. Yet it is not the sort of poetry of ideas which, like Pope's, requires a point of view only. It requires also, for the deepest understanding, which must go beneath the verbal excitement of the style, a highly developed sense of the specific quality of poetry—a quality that most persons accept as the accidental feature of something else that the poet thinks he has to say. This is one reason why Miss Dickinson's poetry has not been widely read.

There is another reason, and it is a part of the problem peculiar to a poetry that comes out of fundamental ideas. We lack a tradition of criticism. There were no points of critical reference passed on to us from a preceding generation. I am not upholding here the so-called dead-hand of tradition, but rather a rational insight into the meaning of the present in terms of some imaginable past implicit in our own lives: we need a body of ideas that can bear upon the course of the spirit and yet remain fixed as a rational instrument. We ignore the present, which is momently translated into the past, and derive our standards from imaginative constructions of the future. The hard contingency of fact invariably breaks these standards down, leaving us the intellectual chaos which is the sore distress of American criticism. Marxian criticism is, I believe, the latest disguise of this heresy.

Still another difficulty stands between us and Miss Dickinson. It is the failure of the scholars to feel more than biographical curiosity about her. We have scholarship, but that is no substitute for a critical tradition. Miss Dickinson's value to the research scholar, who likes historical difficulty for its own sake, is slight; she is too near to possess the remoteness of literature. Perhaps her appropriate setting would be the age of Cowley or of Donne. Yet in her own historical setting she is, nevertheless, remarkable and special.

Although the intellectual climate into which she was born, in 1830, had, as all times have, the features of a transition, the period was also a major crisis culminating

4

in the war between the States. After that war, in New England as well as in the South, spiritual crises were definitely minor until the Great War.

Yet, a generation before the war of 1861–65, the transformation of New England had begun. When Samuel Slater in 1790 thwarted the British embargo on mill-machinery by committing to memory the whole design of a cotton spinner and bringing it to Massachusetts, he planted the seed of the "Western spirit." By 1825 its growth in the East was rank enough to begin choking out the ideas and habits of living that New England along with Virginia had kept in unconscious allegiance to Europe. To the casual observer, perhaps, the New England character of 1830 was largely an eighteenth-century character. But theocracy was on the decline, and industrialism was rising—as Emerson, in an unusually lucid moment put it, "Things are in the saddle." The energy that had built the meeting-house ran the factory.

Now the idea that moved the theocratic state is the most interesting historically of all American ideas. It was, of course, powerful in seventeenth-century England, but in America, where the long arm of Laud could not reach, it acquired an unchecked social and political influence. The important thing to remember about the puritan theocracy is that it permeated, as it could never have done in England, a whole society. It gave final, definite meaning to life, the life of pious and impious, of learned and vulgar alike. It gave—and this is its significance for Emily

Dickinson, and in only slightly lesser degree for Melville and Hawthorne—it gave an heroic proportion and a tragic mode to the experience of the individual. The history of the New England theocracy, from Apostle Eliot to Cotton Mather, is rich in gigantic intellects that broke down—or so it must appear to an outsider—in a kind of moral decadence and depravity. Socially we may not like the New England idea. Yet it had an immense, incalculable value for literature: it dramatized the human soul.

But by 1850 the great fortunes had been made (in the rum, slave, and milling industries), and New England became a museum. The whatnots groaned under the load of knick-knacks, the fine china dogs and cats, the pieces of Oriental jade, the chips off the leaning tower at Pisa. There were the rare books and the cosmopolitan learning. It was all equally displayed as the evidence of a superior culture. The Gilded Age had already begun. But culture, in the true sense, was disappearing. Where the old order, formidable as it was, had held all this personal experience, this eclectic excitement, in a comprehensible whole, the new order tended to flatten it out in a common experience that was not quite in common; it exalted more and more the personal and the unique in the interior sense. Where the old-fashioned puritans got together on a rigid doctrine, and could thus be individualists in manners, the nineteenth-century New Englander, lacking a genuine religious center, began to be a social conformist. The common idea of the Redemption, for example, was replaced by the conformist idea of respectability among neighbors whose spiritual disorder, not very evident at the surface, was becoming acute. A great idea was breaking up, and society was moving towards external uniformity, which is usually the measure of the spiritual sterility inside.

At this juncture Emerson came upon the scene: the Lucifer of Concord, he had better be called hereafter, for he was the light-bearer who could see nothing but light, and was fearfully blind. He looked around and saw the uniformity of life, and called it the routine of tradition, the tyranny of the theological idea. The death of Priam put an end to the hope of Troy, but it was a slight feat of arms for the doughty Pyrrhus; Priam was an old gentleman and almost dead. So was theocracy; and Emerson killed it. In this way he accelerated a tendency that he disliked. It was a great intellectual mistake. By it Emerson unwittingly became the prophet of a piratical industrialism, a consequence of his own wordy individualism that he could not foresee. He hoisted himself on his own petard.

He discredited more than any other man the puritan drama of the soul. The age that followed, from 1865 on, expired in a genteel secularism, a mildly didactic order of feeling whose ornaments were Lowell, Longfellow, and Holmes. "After Emerson had done his work," says Mr. Robert Penn Warren, "any tragic possibilities in that culture were dissipated." Hawthorne alone in his time kept pure, in the primitive terms, the primitive vision; he brings the puritan tragedy to its climax. Man, measured

7

by a great idea outside himself, is found wanting. But for Emerson man is greater than any idea and, being himself the Over-Soul, is innately perfect; there is no struggle because—I state the Emersonian doctrine, which is very slippery, in its extreme terms—because there is no possibility of error. There is no drama in human character because there is no tragic fault. It is not surprising, then, that after Emerson New England literature tastes like a drink of cambric tea. Its very center of vision has disappeared. There is Hawthorne looking back, there is Emerson looking not too clearly at anything ahead: Emily Dickinson, who has in her something of them both, comes in somewhere between.

With the exception of Poe there is no other American poet whose work so steadily emerges, under pressure of certain disintegrating obsessions, from the framework of moral character. There is none of whom it is truer to say that the poet *is* the poetry. Perhaps this explains the zeal of her admirers for her biography; it explains, in part at least, the gratuitous mystery that Mrs. Bianchi, a niece of the poet and her official biographer, has made of her life. The devoted controversy that Miss Josephine Pollitt and Miss Genevieve Taggard a few years ago started with their excellent books shows the extent to which the critics feel the intimate connection of her life and work. Admiration and affection are pleased to linger over the tokens of a great life; but the solution to the Dickinson enigma is peculiarly superior to fact.

The meaning of the identity—which we merely feel—
of character and poetry would be exceedingly obscure,
even if we could draw up a kind of Binet correlation between the two sets of "facts." Miss Dickinson was a recluse;
but her poetry is rich with a profound and varied experience. Where did she get it? Now some of the biographers,
nervous in the presence of this discrepancy, are eager to
find her a love affair, and I think this search is due to a
modern prejudice: we believe that no virgin can know
enough to write poetry. We shall never learn where she
got the rich quality of her mind. The moral image that
we have of Miss Dickinson stands out in every poem; it
is that of a dominating spinster whose very sweetness
must have been formidable. Yet her poetry constantly
moves within an absolute order of truths that overwhelmed her simply because to her they were unalterably-
fixed. It is dangerous to assume that her "life," which to
the biographers means the thwarted love affair she is supposed to have had, gave to her poetry a decisive direction.
It is even more dangerous to suppose that it made her a
poet.

Poets are mysterious, but a poet when all is said is not
much more mysterious than a banker. The critics remain
spellbound by the technical license of her verse and by
the puzzle of her personal life. Personality is a legitimate
interest because it is an incurable interest, but legitimate
as a personal interest only; it will never give up the key
to any one's verse. Used to that end, the interest is false.

"It is apparent," writes Mr. Conrad Aiken, "that Miss Dickinson became a hermit by deliberate and conscious choice"—a sensible remark that we cannot repeat too often. If it were necessary to explain her seclusion with disappointment in love, there would remain the discrepancy between what the seclusion produced and the seclusion looked at as a cause. The effect, which is her poetry, would imply the whole complex of anterior fact, which was the social and religious structure of New England.

The problem to be kept in mind is thus the meaning of her "deliberate and conscious" decision to withdraw from life to her upstairs room. This simple fact is not very important. But that it must have been her sole way of acting out her part in the history of her culture, which made, with the variations of circumstance, a single demand upon all its representatives—this is of the greatest consequence. All pity for Miss Dickinson's "starved life" is misdirected. Her life was one of the richest and deepest ever lived on this continent.

When she went upstairs and closed the door, she mastered life by rejecting it. Others in their way had done it before; still others did it later. If we suppose—which is to suppose the improbable—that the love-affair precipitated the seclusion, it was only a pretext; she would have found another. Mastery of the world by rejecting the world was the doctrine, even if it was not always the practice, of Jonathan Edwards and Cotton Mather. It is the meaning of fate in Hawthorne: his people are fated to withdraw from the world and to be destroyed. And it is the exclusive theme of Henry James.

There is a moral emphasis that connects Hawthorne, James, and Miss Dickinson, and I think it is instructive. Between Hawthorne and James lies an epoch. The temptation to sin, in Hawthorne, is, in James, transformed into the temptation not to do the "decent thing." A whole world-scheme, a complete cosmic background, has shrunk to the dimensions of the individual conscience. This epoch between Hawthorne and James lies in Emerson. James found himself in the post-Emersonian world, and he could not, without violating the detachment proper to an artist, undo Emerson's work; he had that kind of intelligence which refuses to break its head against history. There was left to him only the value, the historic rôle, of rejection. He could merely escape from the physical presence of that world which, for convenience, we may call Emerson's world: he could only take his Americans to Europe upon the vain quest of something that they had lost at home. His characters, fleeing the wreckage of the puritan culture, preserved only their honor. Honor became a sort of forlorn hope struggling against the forces of "pure fact" that got loose in the middle of the century. Honor alone is a poor weapon against nature, being too personal, finical, and proud, and James achieved a victory only by refusing to engage the whole force of the enemy.

In Emily Dickinson the conflict takes place on a vaster field. Now the enemy to all those New Englanders was

Nature, and Miss Dickinson saw into the character of this enemy more deeply than any of the others. The general symbol of Nature, for her, is Death, and her weapon against Death is the entire powerful dumb-show of the puritan theology led by Redemption and Immortality. Morally speaking, the problem for James and Miss Dickinson is similar. But her advantages were greater than his. The advantages lay in the availability to her of the puritan ideas on the theological plane.

These ideas, in her poetry, are momently assailed by the disintegrating force of Nature (appearing as Death) which, while constantly breaking them down, constantly redefines and strengthens them. The values are purified by the triumphant withdrawal from Nature, by their power to recover from Nature. The poet attains to a mastery over experience by facing its utmost implications. There is the clash of powerful opposites, and in all great poetry—for Emily Dickinson is a great poet—it issues in a tension between abstraction and sensation in which the two elements may be, of course, distinguished logically, but not really. We are shown our roots in Nature by examining our differences with Nature; we are renewed by Nature without being delivered into her hands. When it is possible for a poet to do this for us with the greatest imaginative comprehension, a possibility that the poet cannot himself create, we have the perfect literary situation. Only a few times in the history of English poetry has this situation come about, notably, the period between about 1580 and the Restoration. There was a similar age in New England from which emerged two talents of the first order—Hawthorne and Emily Dickinson.

There is an epoch between James and Miss Dickinson. But between her and Hawthorne there exists only a difference of intellectual quality. She lacks almost radically the power to seize upon and understand abstractions for their own sake; she does not separate them from the sensuous illuminations that she is so marvellously adept at; like Donne, she *perceives abstraction* and *thinks sensation*. But Hawthorne was a master of ideas, within a limited range; this narrowness confined him to his own kind of life, his own society, and out of it grew his typical forms of experience, his steady, almost obsessed vision of man; it explains his depth and intensity. Yet he is always conscious of the abstract, doctrinal aspect of his mind, and when his vision of action and emotion is weak, his work becomes didactic. Now Miss Dickinson's poetry often runs into quasi-homiletic forms, but it is never didactic. Her very ignorance, her lack of formal intellectual training, exempted her from the risk that imperilled Hawthorne. She cannot reason at all. She can only *see*. It is impossible to imagine what she might have done with drama or fiction; for, not approaching the puritan temper and through it the puritan myth, through human action, she is able to grasp the terms of the myth directly and by a feat that amounts almost to anthropomorphism, to give them a luminous tension, a kind of drama, among themselves.

One of the perfect poems in English is *The Chariot*,

and it exemplifies better than anything else she wrote the special quality of her mind. I think it will illuminate the tendency of this discussion:

> Because I could not stop for death,
> He kindly stopped for me;
> The carriage held but just ourselves
> And immortality.
>
> We slowly drove, he knew no haste,
> And I had put away
> My labor, and my leisure too,
> For his civility.
>
> We passed the school where children played,
> Their lessons scarcely done;
> We passed the fields of gazing grain,
> We passed the setting sun.
>
> We paused before a house that seemed
> A swelling of the ground;
> The roof was scarcely visible,
> The cornice but a mound.
>
> Since then 'tis centuries; but each
> Feels shorter than the day
> I first surmised the horses' heads
> Were toward eternity.

If the word great means anything in poetry, this poem is one of the greatest in the English language; it is flawless to the last detail. The rhythm charges with movement the pattern of suspended action back of the poem. Every image is precise and, moreover, not merely beautiful, but inextricably fused with the central idea. Every image extends and intensifies every other. The third stanza especially shows Miss Dickinson's power to fuse, into a single order of perception, a heterogeneous series: the children, the grain, and the setting sun (time) have the same degree of credibility; the first subtly preparing for the last. The sharp *gazing* before *grain* instils into nature a kind of cold vitality of which the qualitative richness has infinite depth. The content of death in the poem eludes forever any explicit definition. He is a gentleman taking a lady out for a drive. But note the restraint that keeps the poet from carrying this so far that it is ludicrous and incredible; and note the subtly interfused erotic motive, which the idea of death has presented to every romantic poet, love being a symbol interchangeable with death. The terror of death is objectified through this figure of the genteel driver, who is made ironically to serve the end of Immortality. This is the heart of the poem: she has presented a typical Christian theme in all its final irresolution, without making any final statement about it. There is no solution to the problem; there can be only a statement of it in the full context of intellect and feeling. A construction of the human will, elaborated with all the abstracting powers of the mind, is put to the concrete test of experience: the idea of immortality is confronted with the fact of physical disintegration. We are not told what to think; we are told to look at the situation.

The framework of the poem is, in fact, the two abstractions, mortality and eternity, which are made to associate in perfect equality with the images: she sees the ideas, and thinks the perceptions. She did, of course, nothing of the sort; but we must use the logical distinctions, even to the extent of paradox, if we are to form any notion of this rare quality of mind. She could not in the proper sense think at all, and unless we prefer the feeble poetry of moral ideas that flourished in New England in the eighties, we must conclude that her intellectual deficiency contributed at least negatively to her great distinction. Miss Dickinson is probably the only Anglo-American poet of her century whose work exhibits the perfect literary situation—in which is possible the fusion of sensibility and thought. Unlike her contemporaries, she never succumbed to her ideas, to easy solutions, to her private desires.

Philosophers must deal with ideas, but the trouble with most nineteenth-century poets is too much philosophy; they are nearer to being philosophers than poets, without being in the true sense either. Tennyson is a perfect example of this; so is Arnold in his weak moments. There have been poets like Milton and Donne who were not spoiled for their true business by leaning on a rational system of ideas; that was because they understood the poetic use of their ideas. Tennyson tried to mix a little Huxley and a little Broad Church, without understanding either Broad Church or Huxley; the result was fatal, and what is worse, it was false. Miss Dickinson's ideas were deeply imbedded in her character, not taken from the latest tract. A conscious cultivation of ideas in poetry is always dangerous, and even Milton escaped ruin only by having an instinct for what in the deepest sense he understood. Even at that there is a remote quality in Milton's approach to his material, in his treatment of it; in the nineteenth century, in an imperfect literary situation where literature was confused with documentation, he might have been a pseudo-philosopher-poet. It is impossible to conceive Emily Dickinson and John Donne ever becoming that; they would not have written at all.

Neither the feeling nor the style of Miss Dickinson belongs to the seventeenth century; yet between her and Donne there are remarkable ties. Their religious ideas, their abstractions, are momently toppling from the rational plane to the level of perception. The ideas, in fact, are no longer the impersonal religious symbols created anew in the heat of emotion, that we find in poets like Herbert and Vaughan. They have become, for Donne, the terms of personality; they are mingled with the miscellany of sensation. In Miss Dickinson, as in Donne, we may detect a singularly morbid concern, not for religious truth, but for personal revelation. The modern word is self-exploitation. It is egoism grown irresponsible in religion, and decadent in morals. In religion it is blasphemy; in society it means usually that culture is not self-contained and sufficient, that the spiritual community is breaking up. This is, along with some other features that do not concern us here, the perfect literary situation.

II

Personal revelation of the kind that Donne and Miss Dickinson strove for, in the effort to understand their relation to the world, is a feature of all great poetry; it is probably the hidden motive for writing. It is the effort of the individual to live apart from a cultural tradition that no longer sustains him. But this culture, which I now wish to discuss a little, is indispensable: there is a great deal of shallow nonsense in modern criticism which holds that poetry—and this is a half-truth that is worse than false—is essentially revolutionary. It is only indirectly revolutionary: the intellectual and religious background of an age no longer contains the whole spirit, and the poet proceeds to examine that background in terms of immediate experience. But the background is absolutely necessary; otherwise all the arts, not only poetry, would have to rise in a vacuum. Poetry does not dispense with tradition; it probes the deficiencies of a tradition. But it must have a tradition to probe. It is too bad that Arnold did not explain his doctrine, that poetry is a criticism of life, from the viewpoint of its background: we should have been spared an era of academic misconception, in which criticism of life meant a diluted pragmatism, the criterion of which was respectability. The poet in the true sense "criticizes" his tradition, either as such, or indirectly by comparing it with something that is about to replace it; he does what the root-meaning of the verb implies—

18

he *discerns* its real elements and thus establishes its value, by putting it to the test of experience.

What is the nature of a poet's culture? Or, to put the question properly, what is the meaning of culture for poetry? All the great poets become the material of what we popularly call culture; we study them to acquire it. It is clear that Addison was more cultivated than Shakespeare; nevertheless Shakespeare is a finer source of culture than Addison. What is the meaning of this? Plainly it is that learning has never had anything to do with culture except instrumentally: the poet must be exactly literate enough to write down fully and precisely what he has to say, but no more. The source of a poet's true culture lies back of the paraphernalia of culture, and not all the strenuous activity of this enlightened age can create it.

A culture cannot be consciously created. It is an available source of ideas that are imbedded in a complete and homogeneous society. The poet finds himself balanced upon the moment when such a world is about to fall, when it threatens to run out into looser and less self-sufficient impulses. This world order is assimilated, in Miss Dickinson, as mediævalism was in Shakespeare, to the poetic vision; it is brought down from abstraction to personal sensibility.

Now in this connection it may be said that the prior conditions for great poetry, given a great talent, are just two: the thoroughness of the poet's discipline in an objective system of truth, and his lack of consciousness of such a discipline. For this discipline is a number of fundamental ideas the origin of which the poet does not know; they give form and stability to his fresh perceptions of the world; and he cannot shake them off. This is his culture, and like Tennyson's God it is nearer than hands and feet. With reasonable certainty we unearth the elements of Shakespeare's culture, and yet it is equally certain—so innocent was he of his own resources—that he would not know what our discussion is about. He appeared at the collapse of the mediæval system as a rigid pattern of life, but that pattern remained in Shakespeare what Shelley called a "fixed point of reference" for his sensibility. Miss Dickinson, as we have seen, was born into the equilibrium of an old and a new order. Puritanism could not be to her what it had been to the generation of Cotton Mather—a body of absolute truths; it was an unconscious discipline timed to the pulse of her life.

The perfect literary situation—that is what it is: it produces, because it is rare, a special and perhaps the most distinguished kind of poet. I am not trying to invent a new critical category. Such poets are never very much alike on the surface; they show us all the varieties of poetic feeling; and like other poets they resist all classification but that of temporary convenience. But, I believe, Miss Dickinson and John Donne would have this in common: their sense of the natural world is not blunted by a too rigid system of ideas; yet the ideas, the abstractions, their education or their intellectual heritage, are not so weak as to let their immersion in nature, or their purely personal quality, get out of control. The two poles of the mind are not separately visible; we infer them from the lucid tension that may be most readily illustrated by polar activity. There is no thought as such at all; nor is there feeling; there is that unique focus of experience which is at once neither and both.

Like Miss Dickinson, Shakespeare has no opinions whatever; his peculiar merit too is deeply involved in his failure to think about anything; his meaning is not in the content of his expression; it is in the tension of the dramatic relations of his characters. This kind of poetry is at the opposite of intellectualism. (Miss Dickinson is obscure and difficult, but that is not intellectualism.) To T. W. Higginson, the editor of *The Atlantic Monthly,* who tried to advise her, she wrote that she had no education. In any sense that Higginson could understand, it was quite true. His kind of education was the conscious cultivation of abstractions. She did not reason about the world she saw; she merely saw it. The "ideas" implicit in the world within her rose up, concentrated in her slightest perception.

That kind of world at present has for us something of the fascination of a buried city. There is none like it. When such worlds exist, when such cultures flourish, they support not only the poet but all members of society. For, from these, the poet differs only in his gift for exhibiting the structure, the internal lineaments, of his culture by threatening to tear them apart: a process that concentrates the symbolic emotions of society while it seems to attack them. The poet may hate his age; he may be an outcast like Villon; but this world is always there as the background to what he has to say. It is the lens through which he brings nature to focus and control— the clarifying medium that concentrates his personal feeling. It is ready-made; he cannot make it; with it, his poetry has a spontaneity and a certainty of direction that, without it, it would lack. No poet could have invented the elements of *The Chariot;* only a great poet could have used them so perfectly. Miss Dickinson was a deep mind writing from a deep culture, and when she came to poetry, she came infallibly.

Infallibly, at her best; for no poet has ever been perfect, nor is Emily Dickinson. Her unsurpassed precision of statement is due to the directness with which the abstract framework of her thought acts upon its unorganized material. The two elements of her style, considered as point of view, are immortality, or the idea of permanence, and the physical process of death or decay. Her diction has two corresponding features: words of Latin or Greek origin and, sharply opposed to these, the concrete Saxon element. It is this verbal conflict that gives to her verse its high tension; it is not a device deliberately seized upon, but a feeling for language that senses out the two fundamental components of English and their metaphysical relation: the Latin for ideas and the Saxon for perceptions—the peculiar virtue of English as a poetic tongue. Only the great poets know how to use this advantage of our language.

Like all poets, Miss Dickinson often writes out of habit;

the style that emerged from some deep exploration of an idea is carried on as verbal habit when she has nothing to say. She indulges herself:

> There's something quieter than sleep
> Within this inner room!
> It wears a sprig upon its breast,
> And will not tell its name.
>
> Some touch it and some kiss it,
> Some chafe its idle hand;
> It has a simple gravity
> I do not understand!
>
> While simple hearted neighbors
> Chat of the 'early dead,'
> We, prone to periphrasis,
> Remark that birds have fled!

It is only a pert remark; at best a superior kind of punning—one of the worst specimens of her occasional interest in herself.

But she never had the slightest interest in the public. Were four poems or five published in her lifetime? She never felt the temptation to round off a poem for public exhibition. Higginson's kindly offer to make her verse "correct" was an invitation to throw her work into the public ring—the ring of Lowell and Longfellow. He could not see that he was tampering with one of the rarest literary integrities of all time. Here was a poet who had no use for the supports of authorship—flattery and fame; she never needed money.

She had all the elements of a culture that has broken up, a culture that on the religious side takes its place in the museum of spiritual antiquities. Puritanism, as a unified version of the world, is dead; only a remnant of it in trade may be said to survive. In the history of puritanism she comes between Hawthorne and Emerson. She has Hawthorne's matter, which a too irresponsible personality tends to dilute into a form like Emerson's; she is often betrayed by words. But she is not the poet of personal sentiment; she has more to say than she can put down in any one poem. Like Hardy and Whitman she must be read entire; like Shakespeare she never gives up her meaning in a single line.

She is therefore a perfect subject for the kind of criticism which is chiefly concerned with general ideas. She exhibits one of the permanent relations between personality and objective truth, and she deserves the special attention of our time, which lacks that kind of truth.

She has Hawthorne's intellectual toughness, a hard, definite sense of the physical world. The highest flights to God, the most extravagant metaphors of the strange and the remote, come back to a point of casuistry, to a moral dilemma of the experienced world. There is, in spite of the homiletic vein of utterance, no abstract speculation, nor is there a message to society; she speaks wholly to the individual experience. She offers to the unimaginative no riot of vicarious sensation; she has no useful maxims for men of action. Up to this point her resemblance to Emerson is slight: poetry is a sufficient form of utterance, and her devotion to it is pure. But in Emily Dickinson the puritan world is no longer self-contained; it is no longer complete; her sensibility exceeds its dimensions. She has trimmed down its supernatural proportions; it has become a morality; instead of the tragedy of the spirit there is a commentary upon it. Her poetry is a magnificent personal confession, blasphemous and, in its self-revelation, its implacable honesty, almost obscene. It comes out of an intellectual life towards which it feels no moral responsibility. Mather would have burnt her for a witch.

II. Hart Crane

THE career of Hart Crane will be written by future critics as a chapter in the neo-symbolist movement. An historical view of his poetry at this time would be misleading and incomplete. Like most poets of his age in America, Crane discovered Rimbaud through Eliot and the Imagists; it is certain that long before he had done any of his best work he had come to believe himself the spiritual heir of the French poet. While it is true that he mastered the symbolist use of fused metaphor, it is also true that this is a feature of all poetic language. Whether Crane's style is symbolistic, or should, in many instances, like the first six or seven stanzas of *The River,* be called Elizabethan, is a question that need not concern us now.

Between *The Bridge* and *Une Saison d'Enfer* there is little essential affinity. Rimbaud achieved "disorder" out of implicit order, after a deliberate cultivation of "derangement," but in our time the disintegration of our intellectual systems is accomplished. With Crane the disorder is original and fundamental. That is the special quality of his mind that belongs peculiarly to our own time. His æsthetic problem, however, was more general; it was the historic problem of romanticism.

Harold Hart Crane, one of the great masters of the romantic movement, was born in Garrettsville, Ohio, on

July 21, 1899. His birthplace is a small town near Cleveland, in the old Western Reserve, a region which, as distinguished from the lower portions of the state, where people from the Southern up-country settled, was populated largely by New England stock. He seems to have known little of his ancestry, but he frequently said that his maternal forbears had given Hartford, Connecticut, its name, and that they went "back to Stratford-on-Avon" —a fiction surely, but one that gave him distinct pleasure. His formal education was slight. After the third year at high school, when he was fifteen, it ended, and he worked in his father's candy factory in Cleveland, where the family had removed in his childhood. He repeatedly told me that money had been set aside for his education at college, but that it had been used for other purposes. With the instinct of genius he read the great poets, but he never acquired an objective mastery of any literature, or even of the history of his country—a defect of considerable interest in a poet whose most ambitious work is an American epic.

In any ordinary sense Crane was not an educated man; in many respects he was an ignorant man. There is already a Crane legend, like the Poe legend—it should be fostered because it will help to make his poetry generally known—and the scholars will decide it was a pity that so great a talent lacked early advantages. It is probable that he was incapable of the formal discipline of a classical education, and probable, too, that the eclectic education of his time would have scattered and killed his talent.

His poetry not only has defects of the surface, it has a defect of vision; but its great and peculiar value cannot be separated from its limitations. Its qualities are bound up with a special focus of the intellect and sensibility, and it would be foolish to wish that his mind had been better trained or differently organized.

The story of his suicide is well known. The information that I have seems authentic, but it is incomplete and subject to excessive interpretation. Toward the end of April, 1932, he embarked on the S.S. *Orizaba* bound from Vera Cruz to New York. On the night of April 26 he got into a brawl with some sailors; he was severely beaten and robbed. At noon the next day, the ship being in the Caribbean a few hours out of Havana, he rushed from his stateroom clad in pajamas and overcoat, walked through the smoking-room out onto the deck, and then the length of the ship to the stern. There without hesitation he made a perfect dive into the sea. It is said that a life-preserver was thrown to him; he either did not see it or did not want it. By the time the ship had turned back he had disappeared. Whether he forced himself down—for a moment he was seen swimming—or was seized by a shark, as the captain believed, cannot be known. After a search of thirty-five minutes his body was not found, and the *Orizaba* put back into her course.

In the summer of 1930 he had written to me that he feared his most ambitious work, *The Bridge,* was not quite perfectly "realized," that probably his soundest work was in the shorter pieces of *White Buildings,* but that his mind, being once committed to the larger undertaking, could never return to the lyrical and more limited form. He had an extraordinary insight into the foundations of his work, and I think this judgment of it will not be refuted.

From 1922 to 1928—after that year I saw him and heard from him irregularly until his death—I could observe the development of his style from poem to poem; and his letters—written always in a pure and lucid prose —provide a valuable commentary on his career. This is not the place to bring all this material together for judgment. As I look back upon his work and its relation to the life he lived, a general statement about it comes to my mind that may throw some light on the dissatisfaction that he felt with his career. It will be a judgment upon the life and works of a man whom I knew for ten years as a friend.

Suicide was the sole act of will left to him short of a profound alteration of his character. I think the evidence of this is the locked-in sensibility, the insulated egoism, of his poetry—a subject that I shall return to. The background of his death was dramatically perfect: a large portion of his finest imagery was of the sea, chiefly the Caribbean:

> O minstrel galleons of Carib fire,
> Bequeath us to no earthly shore until
> Is answered in the vortex of our grave
> The seal's wide spindrift gaze towards paradise.

His verse is full of splendid images of this order, a rich

symbolism for an implicit pantheism that, whatever may be its intrinsic merit, he had the courage to vindicate with death in the end.

His pantheism was not passive and contemplative; it rose out of the collision between his own locked-in sensibility and the ordinary forms of experience. Every poem is a thrust of that sensibility into the world: his defect lay in his inability to face out the moral criticism implied in the failure to impose his will upon experience.

The Bridge is presumably an epic. How early he had conceived the idea of the poem and the leading symbolism, it is difficult to know; certainly as early as February, 1923. Up to that time, with the exception of *For the Marriage of Faustus and Helen* (1922), he had written only short poems, but most of them, *Praise for an Urn, Black Tambourine, Paraphrase,* and *Emblems of Conduct,* are among his finest work. It is a mistake then to suppose that all of *White Buildings* is early experimental writing; a large portion of that volume, and perhaps the least successful part of it, is made up of poems written after *The Bridge* was begun. *Praise for an Urn* was written in the spring of 1922—one of the finest elegies by an American poet—and although his later development gave us a poetry that the period would be much the less rich for not having, he never again had such perfect mastery of his subject—because he never again knew precisely what his subject was.

Readers familiar with *For the Marriage of Faustus and Helen* admire it by passages, but the form of the poem, in its framework of symbol, is an abstraction empty of any knowable experience. It is a conventional revival of the kind of diction that a young poet picks up in his first reading. Crane, I believe, felt that this was so; and he became so dissatisfied, not only with the style of the poem, which is heavily influenced by Eliot and Laforgue, but with the "literary" character of the symbolism, that he set about the greater task of writing *The Bridge*. He had looked upon his *Faustus and Helen* as an answer to the cultural pessimism of the school of Eliot, and *The Bridge* was to be an even more complete answer.

There was a fundamental mistake in Crane's diagnosis of Eliot's problem. Eliot's "pessimism" grows out of an awareness of the decay of the individual consciousness and its fixed relations to the world; but Crane thought that it was due to something like pure "orneryness," an unwillingness "to share with us the breath released," the breath being a new kind of freedom that he identified emotionally with the age of the machine. This vagueness of purpose, in spite of the apparently concrete character of the Brooklyn Bridge, which became the symbol of his epic, he never succeeded in correcting. The "bridge" stands for no well-defined experience; it differs from the Helen and Faust symbols only in its unliterary origin. I think Crane was deceived by this difference, and by the fact that Brooklyn Bridge is "modern" and a fine piece of "mechanics." His more ambitious later project permitted him no greater degree of formal structure than the more literary symbolism of his youth.

The fifteen parts of *The Bridge* taken as one poem suffer from the lack of a coherent structure, whether symbolic or narrative: the coherence of the work consists in the personal quality of the writing—in mood, feeling, and tone. In the best passages Crane has perfect mastery over the quality of his style; but it lacks an objective pattern of ideas elaborate enough to carry it through an epic or heroic work. The single symbolic image, in which the whole poem centers, is at one moment the actual Brooklyn Bridge; at another, it is any bridge or "connection"; at still another, it is a philosophical pun and becomes the basis of a series of analogies.

In *Cape Hatteras,* the aëroplane and Walt Whitman are analogous "bridges" to some transcendental truth. Because the idea is variously metaphor, symbol, and analogy, it tends to make the poem static. The poet takes it up, only to be forced to put it down again *when the poetic image of the moment is exhausted.* The idea does not, in short, fill the poet's mind; it is the starting point for a series of short flights, or inventions connected only in analogy—which explains the merely personal passages, which are obscure, and the lapses into sentimentality. For poetic sentimentality is emotion undisciplined by the structure of events or ideas of which it is ostensibly a part. The idea is not objective and articulate in itself; it lags after the poet's vision; it appears and disappears; and in the intervals Crane improvises, often beautifully, as in the flight of the aëroplane, sometimes badly, as in the passage on Whitman in the same poem.

In the great epic and philosophical works of our tradition, notably the *Divine Comedy,* the intellectual
groundwork is not only simple philosophically; we not
only know that the subject is personal salvation, just as
we know that Crane's is the greatness of America: we
are given also the complete articulation of the idea down
to the slightest detail, and we are given it objectively
apart from anything that the poet is going to say about it.
When the poet extends his perception, there is a further
extension of the groundwork ready to meet it and discipline it, and to compel the sensibility of the poet to
stick to the subject. It is a game of chess; neither side can
move without consulting the other. Crane's difficulty is
that of modern poets generally: they play the game with
half of the men, the men of sensibility, and because sensibility can make any move, the significance of all moves
is obscure.

If we subtract from Crane's idea its periphery of sensation, we have left only the dead abstraction, the Greatness of America, which is capable of elucidation neither
on the logical plane nor in terms of a generally accepted
idea of America.

The theme of *The Bridge* is, in fact, an emotional over-
simplification of a subject-matter that Crane did not, on
the plane of narrative and idea, simplify at all. The poem
is emotionally homogeneous and simple—it contains a
single purpose; but because it is not structurally clarified
it is emotionally confused. America stands for a passage
into new truths. Is this the meaning of American his-

tory? The poet has every right to answer yes, and this he has done. But just what in America or about America stands for this? Which American history? The historical plot of the poem, which is the groundwork on which the symbolic bridge stands, is arbitrary and broken, where the poet would have gained an overwhelming advantage by choosing a single period or episode, a concrete event with all its dramatic causes, and by following it up minutely, and being bound to it. In short, he would have gained an advantage could he have found a subject to stick to.

Does American culture afford such a subject? It probably does not. After the seventeenth century the sophisticated history of the scholars came into fashion; our popular, legendary chronicles come down only from the remoter European past. It was a sound impulse on Crane's part to look for an American myth, some simple version of our past that lies near the center of the American consciousness; an heroic tale with just enough symbolism to give his mind both direction and play. The soundness of his purpose is witnessed also by the kind of history in the poem: it is inaccurate, and it will not at all satisfy the sticklers for historical fact. It is the history of the motion picture, of naïve patriotism. This is sound; for it ignores the scientific ideal of historical truth-in-itself, and looks for a cultural truth which might win the spontaneous allegiance of the people. It is on such simple integers of truth, not truth of fact but of religious necessity, that men unite. The American mind was formed by the eighteenth-century Enlightenment, which broke down the European truths and gave us a temper deeply hostile to the making of new religious truths of our own.

The impulse in *The Bridge* is religious, but the soundness of an impulse is no warrant that it will create a sound art form. The form depends on too many factors beyond the control of the poet. The age is scientific and pseudo-scientific, and our philosophy is Doctor Dewey's instrumentalism. And it is possibly this circumstance that has driven the religious attitude into a corner where it lacks the right instruments for its defense and growth, and where it is in a vast muddle about just what these instruments are. Perhaps this disunity of the intellect is responsible for Crane's unphilosophical belief that the poet, unaided and isolated from the people, can create a myth.

If anthropology has helped to destroy the credibility of myths, it has shown us how they rise: their growth is mysterious from the people as a whole. It is probable that no one man ever put myth into history. It is still a nice problem among higher critics, whether the authors of the Gospels were deliberate myth-makers, or whether their minds were simply constructed that way; but the evidence favors the latter. Crane was a myth-maker, and in an age favorable to myths he would have written a mythical poem in the act of writing an historical one.

It is difficult to agree with those critics who find his epic a single poem and as such an artistic success. It is a collection of lyrics, the best of which are not surpassed by

35

anything in American literature. The writing is most distinguished when Crane is least philosophical, *when he writes from sensation. The River* has some blemishes towards the end, but by and large it is a masterpiece of order and style; it alone is enough to place Crane in the first rank of American poets, living or dead. Equally good but less ambitious are the *Proem: To Brooklyn Bridge,* and *Harbor Dawn,* and *The Dance* from the section called *Powhatan's Daughter.*

These poems bear only the loosest relation to the symbolic demands of the theme; they contain allusions to the historical pattern or extend the slender structure of analogy running through the poem. They are primarily lyrical, and each has its complete form. The poem *Indiana,* written presumably to complete the pattern of *Powhatan's Daughter,* does not stand alone, and it is one of the most astonishing performances ever made by a poet of Crane's genius. *The Dance* gives us the American background for the coming white man, and *Indiana* carries the stream of history to the pioneer West. It is a nightmare of sentimentality. Crane is at his most "philosophical" in a theme in which he feels no poetic interest whatever.

The structural defect of *The Bridge* is due to this fundamental contradiction of purpose. In one of his best earlier poems, *The Wine Menagerie,* he exclaims: "New thresholds, new anatomies!"—new sensation, but he could not subdue the new sensation to a symbolic form.

His pantheism is necessarily a philosophy of sensation without point of view. An epic is a judgment of human action, an implied evaluation of a civilization, a way of life. In *The Bridge* the civilization that contains the subway hell of the section called *The Tunnel* is the same civilization of the aëroplane that the poet apostrophizes in *Cape Hatteras:* there is no reason why the subway should be a fitter symbol of damnation than the aëroplane: both were produced by the same mentality on the same moral plane. There is a concealed, meaningless analogy between, on the one hand, the height of the plane and the depth of the subway, and, on the other, "higher" and "lower" in the religious sense. At one moment Crane faces his predicament of blindness to any rational order of value, and knows that he is damned; but he cannot face it long, and he tries to rest secure upon the intensity of sensation.

To the vision of the abyss in *The Tunnel,* a vision that Dante passed through midway of this mortal life, Crane had no alternative: when it became too harrowing he cried to his Pocahontas, a typically romantic and sentimental symbol:

Lie to us—dance us back our tribal morn!

It is probably the perfect word of romanticism in this century. When Crane saw that his leading symbol, the bridge, would not hold all the material of his poem, he could not sustain it ironically, in the classical manner, by probing its defects; nor in the personal sections, like *Quaker Hill,* does he include himself in his Leopardian denunciation of life. He is the blameless victim of a world whose impurity violates the moment of intensity, which would otherwise be enduring and perfect. He is betrayed, not by a defect of his own nature, but by the external world; he asks of nature, perfection—requiring only of himself, intensity. The persistent, and persistently defeated, pursuit of a natural absolute places Crane at the center of his age.

Alternately he asserts the symbol of the bridge and abandons it, because fundamentally he does not understand it. The idea of bridgeship is an elaborate blur leaving the inner structure of the poem confused.

Yet some of the best poetry of our times is in *The Bridge*. Its inner confusion is a phase of the inner cross-purposes of the time. Crane was one of those men whom every age seems to select as the spokesmen of its spiritual life; they give the age away. The accidental features of their lives, their place in life, their very heredity, seem to fit them for their rôle; even their vices contribute to their preparation. Crane's biographer will have to study the early influences that confirmed him in narcissism, and thus made him typical of the rootless spiritual life of our time. The character formed by those influences represents an immense concentration, and becomes almost a symbol, of American life in this age.

Crane's poetry has incalculable moral value: it reveals our defects in their extremity. I have said that he knew little of the history of his country. It was not a mere defect of education, but a defect, in the spiritual sense, of the modern mind. Professor Charles A. Beard has immense information about American history, but understands almost none of it: Crane lacked the sort of indispensable understanding of his country that a New England farmer has who has never been out of his township. *The Bridge* attempts to include all American life, but it covers the ground with seven-league boots and, like a sightseer, sees nothing. With reference to its leading symbol, it has no subject-matter. The poem is the effort of a solipsistic sensibility to locate itself in the external world, to establish points of reference.

It seems to me that by testing out his capacity to construct a great objective piece of work, in which his definition of himself should have been perfectly articulated, he brought his work to an end. I think he knew that the structure of *The Bridge* was finally incoherent, and for that reason—as I have said—he could no longer believe in even his lyrical powers; he could not return to the early work and take it up where he had left off. Far from "refuting" Eliot, his whole career is a vindication of Eliot's major premise—that the integrity of the individual consciousness has broken down. Crane had, in his later work, no individual consciousness: the hard firm style of *Praise for an Urn,* which is based upon a clear-cut perception of moral relations, and upon their ultimate inviolability, begins to disappear when the poet goes out into the world and finds that the simplicity of a child's world has no universal sanction. From then on, instead of the effort to define himself in the midst of almost overwhelming complications—a situation that might have produced a tragic poet—he falls back upon the intensity

39

of consciousness, rather than the clarity, for his center of vision. And that is romanticism.

His world had no center, and the compensatory action that he took is responsible for the fragmentary quality of his most ambitious work. This action took two forms— the blind assertion of the will, and the blind desire for self-destruction. The poet did not face his first problem, which is to define the limits of his personality and to objectify its moral implications in an appropriate symbolism. Crane could only assert a quality of will against the world, and at each successive failure of the will he turned upon himself. In the failure of understanding—and understanding, for Dante, was a way of love—the romantic modern poet of the age of science attempts to impose his will upon experience and to possess the world.

It is this impulse of the modern period that has given us the greatest romantic poetry: Crane instinctively continued the conception of the will that was the deliberate discovery of Rimbaud. A poetry of the will is a poetry of sensation, for the poet surrenders to his sensations of the object in his effort to identify himself with it, and to own it. Some of Crane's finest lyrics—those written in the period of *The Bridge*—carry the modern impulse as far as you will find it anywhere in the French romantics. *Lachrymae Christi* and *Passage,* though on the surface made up of pure images without philosophical meaning of the explicit sort in *The Bridge,* are the lyrical equivalents of the epic: the same kind of sensibility is at work. The implicit grasp of his material that we find in *Praise for an Urn,* the poet has exchanged for an external, random symbol of which there is no possibility of realization. *The Bridge* is an irrational symbol of the will, of conquest, of blind achievement in space; its obverse is *Passage,* whose lack of external symbolism exhibits the poetry of the will on the plane of sensation; and this is the self-destructive return of the will upon itself.

Criticism may well set about isolating the principle upon which Crane's poetry is organized. Powerful verse overwhelms its admirers, and betrays them into more than technical imitation. That is one of the arguments of Platonism against literature; it is the immediate quality of an art rather than its whole significance, that sets up schools and traditions. Crane not only ends the romantic era in his own person; he ends it logically and morally. Beyond Crane no future poet can go. (This does not mean that the romantic impulse may not rise and flourish again.) The finest passages in his work are single moments in the stream of sensation; beyond the moment he goes at peril; for outside it there lies the discrepancy between the sensuous fact, the perception, and its organizing symbol—a discrepancy that plunges him into chaos and sentimentality. A true symbol has in it, within the terms of its properties, all the qualities that the artist is able to attribute to it. But the "bridge" is empty and static, it has no inherent content, and the poet's attribution to it of the qualities of his own moral predicament is arbitrary. That explains the fragmentary and often unintelligible framework of the poem. There was neither complete action nor ordered symbolism in terms of which the distinct moments of perception could be clarified.

This was partly the problem of Rimbaud. But Crane's problem was nearer to the problem of Keats, and *The Bridge* is a failure in the sense that *Hyperion* is a failure, and with comparable magnificence. Crane's problem, being farther removed from the epic tradition, was actually more difficult than Keats's, and his treatment of it was doubtless the most satisfactory possible in our time. Beyond the quest of pure sensation and its ordering symbolism lies the total destruction of art. By attempting an extreme solution of the romantic problem Crane proved that it cannot be solved.

III. Ezra Pound

I

and as for text we have taken it
from that of Messire Laurentius
and from a codex once of the Lords Malatesta. . . .

ONE is not certain who Messire Laurentius was; one is not very certain that it makes no difference. Yet one takes comfort in the vast range of Mr. Pound's obscure learning, which no one man could be expected to know much about. In his great work one is continually uncertain, as to space, time, history. The codex of the Lords Malatesta is less disconcerting than Laurentius; for more than half of the thirty cantos* contain long paraphrases or garbled quotations from the correspondence, public and private, of the Renaissance Italians, chiefly Florentine and Venetian. About a third of the lines are versified documents. Another third are classical allusions, esoteric quotations from the ancients, fragments of the Greek poets with bits of the Romans thrown in; all magnificently written into Mr. Pound's own text. The rest is contemporary—anecdotes, satirical pictures of vulgar Americans, obscene stories, evenings in low Mediterranean dives, and gossip about intrigants behind the scenes of European power. The three kinds of material in the cantos are antiquity, the Renaissance, and the modern

* *A Draft of XXX Cantos.* By Ezra Pound. Farrar and Rinehart. New York, 1933.

43

world. They are combined on no principle that seems in the least consistent to a first glance. They appear to be mixed in an incoherent jumble, or to stand up in puzzling contrasts.

This is the poetry which, in early and incomplete editions, has had more influence on us than any other of our time; it has had an immense "underground" reputation. And deservedly. For even the early reader of Mr. Pound could not fail to detect the presence of a new poetic form in the individual cantos, though the full value and intention of this form appears for the first time in the complete work. It is not that there is any explicit feature of the whole design that is not contained in each canto; it is simply that Mr. Pound must be read in bulk; it is only then that the great variety of his style and the apparent incoherence turn into implicit order and form. There is no other poetry like the *Cantos* in English. And there is none quite so simple in form. The form is in fact so simple that almost no one has guessed it, and I suppose it will continue to puzzle, perhaps to enrage, our more academic critics for a generation to come. But this form by virtue of its simplicity remains inviolable to critical terms: even now it cannot be technically described.

I begin to talk like Mr. Pound, or rather in the way in which most readers think Mr. Pound writes. The secret of his form is this: conversation. The cantos are talk, talk, talk; not by any one in particular to any one else in particular; they are just rambling talk. At least each canto is a cunningly devised imitation of a casual conversation in which no one presses any subject very far. The length of breath, the span of conversational energy, is the length of a canto. The conversationalist pauses; there is just enough unfinished business left hanging in the air to give him a new start; so that the transitions between the cantos are natural and easy.

Each canto has the broken flow and the somewhat elusive climax of a good monologue: because there is no single speaker, it is a many-voiced monologue. That is the method of the poems—though there is another quality of the form that I must postpone for a moment— *and that is what the poems are about.*

There are, as I have said, three subjects of conversation —ancient times, Renaissance Italy, and the present—but these are not what the cantos are about. They are not about Italy, nor about Greece, nor are they about us. They are not about anything. But they are distinguished verse. Mr. Pound himself tells us:

> And they want to know what we talked about?
> *"de litteris et de armis, praestantibus ingeniis,*
> Both of ancient times and our own; books, arms,
> And men of unusual genius
> Both of ancient times and our own, in short the usual
>   subjects
> Of conversation between intelligent men."

II

There is nothing in the cantos more difficult than that. There is nothing inherently obscure; nothing too profound for any reader who has enough information to get to the background of the allusions in a learned conversation. But there is something that no reader, short of some years of hard textual study, will understand. This is the very heart of the cantos, the secret of Mr. Pound's poetic character, which will only gradually emerge from a detailed analysis of every passage. And this is no more than our friends are constantly demanding of us; we hear them talk, and we return to hear them talk, we return to hear them again, but we never know what they talk about; we return for the mysterious quality of charm that has no rational meaning that we can define. It is only after a long time that the order, the direction, the rhythm of the talker's mind, the logic of his character as distinguished from anything logical he may say—it is a long time before this begins to take on form for us. So with Mr. Pound's cantos. It is doubtless easier for us (who are trained in the more historic brands of poetry) when the poems are about God, Freedom, and Immortality, but there is no reason why poetry should not be so perplexingly simple as Mr. Pound's, and be about nothing at all.

The ostensible subjects of the cantos—ancient, middle, and modern times—are only the materials round which Mr. Pound's mind plays constantly; they are the screen upon which he throws a flowing quality of poetic thought. Now in conversation the memorable quality is a sheer accident of character, and is not designed; but in the cantos the effect is deliberate, and from the first canto to the thirtieth the set tone is maintained without a lapse.

It is this tone, it is this quality quite simply which is

the meaning of the cantos, and although, as I have said, it is simple and direct, it is just as hard to pin down, it is as hidden in its shifting details, as a running, ever-changing conversation. It cannot be taken out of the text; and yet the special way that Mr. Pound has of weaving his three materials together, of emphasizing them, of comparing and contrasting them, gives us a clue to the leading intention of the poems. I come to that quality of the form which I postponed.

The easiest interpretation of all poetry is the allegorical: there are few poems that cannot be paraphrased into a kind of symbolism, which is usually false, being by no means the chief intention of the poet. It is very probable, therefore, that I am about to falsify the true simplicity of the cantos into a simplicity that is merely convenient and spurious. The reader must bear this in mind, and view the slender symbolism that I am going to read into the cantos as a critical shorthand, useful perhaps, but which when used must be dropped.

One of the finest cantos is properly the first. It describes a voyage:

> And then went down to the ship,
> Set keel to breakers, forth on the godly sea, and
> We set up mast and sail on that swart ship,
> Bore sheep aboard her, and our bodies also
> Heavy with weeping, and winds from sternward
> Bore us out onward with bellying canvas,
> Circe's this craft, the trim-coifed goddess.

They land, having come "to the place aforesaid by Circe"

—whatever place it may be—and Tiresias appears, who
says:

> "Odysseus
> Shall return through spiteful Neptune, over dark seas,
> Lose all companions." And then Anticlea came.
> Lie quiet Divus. I mean, that is, Andreas Divus,
> In officina Wecheli, 1538, out of Homer.
> And he sailed, by Sirens and thence outward and away
> And unto Circe.

Mr. Pound's world is the scene of a great Odyssey, and
everywhere he lands it is the shore of Circe, where men
"lose all companions" and are turned into swine. It would
not do at all to push this hint too far, but I will risk one
further point: Mr. Pound is a typically modern, rootless,
and internationalized intelligence. In the place of the traditional supernaturalism of the older and local cultures,
he has a cosmopolitan curiosity that seeks out marvels,
which are all equally marvellous, whether it be a Greek
myth or the antics in Europe of a lady from Kansas. He
has the bright, cosmopolitan *savoir faire* which refuses to
be "taken in": he will not believe, being a traditionalist
at bottom, that the "perverts, who have set money-lust
before the pleasures of the senses," are better than swine.
And ironically, being modern and a hater of modernity,
he sees all history as deformed by the trim-coifed god-
dess.

The cantos are a book of marvels—marvels that he has
read about, or heard of, or seen; there are Greek myths,
tales of Italian feuds, meetings with strange people, ru-
mors of intrigues of state, memories of remarkable dead

friends like T. E. Hulme, comments on philosophical problems, harangues on abuses of the age; the "usual subjects of conversation between intelligent men."

It is all fragmentary. Now nearly every canto begins with a bit of heroic antiquity, some myth, or classical quotation, or a lovely piece of lyrical description in a grand style. It invariably breaks down. It trails off into a piece of contemporary satire, or a flat narrative of the rascality of some Italian prince. This is the special quality of Mr. Pound's form, the essence of his talk, the direction of these magnificent conversations.

For not once does Mr. Pound give himself up to any single story or myth. The thin symbolism from the Circe myth is hardly more than a leading tone, an unconscious prejudice about men which he is not willing to indicate beyond the barest outline. He cannot believe in myths, much less in his own power of imagining them out to a conclusion. None of his myths is compelling enough to draw out his total intellectual resources; none goes far enough to become a belief or even a momentary fiction. They remain marvels to be looked at, but they are meaningless, the wrecks of civilization. His powerful juxtapositions of the ancient, the Renaissance, and the modern worlds reduce all three elements to an unhistorical miscellany, timeless and without origin, and no longer a force in the lives of men.

III

And that is the peculiarly modern quality of Mr. Pound. There is a certain likeness in this to another book of marvels, stories of antiquity known to us as *The Golden Ass.* The cantos are a sort of *Golden Ass.* There is a likeness, but there is no parallel beyond the mere historical one: both books are the productions of worlds without convictions and given over to a hard pragmatism. Here the similarity ends. For Mr. Pound is a powerful reactionary, a faithful mind devoted to those ages when the myths were not merely pretty, but true. And there is a cloud of melancholy irony hanging over the *Cantos.* He is persuaded that the myths are only beautiful, and he drops them after a glimpse, but he is not reconciled to this æstheticism: he ironically puts the myths against the ugly specimens of modern life that have defeated them. But neither are the specimens of modernity worthy of the dignity of belief:

> She held that a sonnet was a sonnet
> And ought never to be destroyed
> And had taken a number of courses
> And continued with hope of degrees and
> Ended in a Baptist learnery
> Somewhere near the Rio Grande.

I am not certain that Mr. Pound will agree with me that he is a traditionalist; nor am I convinced that Mr. Pound, for his part, is certain of anything but his genius for poetry. He is probably one of two or three living Americans who will be remembered as poets of the first order. Yet there is no reason to infer from that that Mr. Pound, outside his craft (or outside his written conversation) knows in the least what he is doing or saying. He is and always has been in a muddle of revolution; and for some appalling reason he identifies his crusade with liberty—liberty of speech, liberty of press, liberty of conduct—in short, liberty. I do not mean to say that either Mr. Pound or his critic knows what liberty is. Nevertheless, Mr. Pound identifies it with civilization and intelligence of the modern and scientific variety. And yet the ancient cultures, which he so much admires, were, from any modern viewpoint, hatched in barbarism and superstition. One is entitled to the suspicion that Mr. Pound prefers barbarism, and that by taking up the rôle of revolution against it he has bitten off his nose to spite his face. He is the confirmed enemy of provincialism, never suspecting that his favorite, Lorenzo the Magnificent, for example, was provincial to the roots of his hair.

The confusion runs through the *Cantos*. It makes the irony that I have spoken of partly unconscious. For as the apostle of humane culture, he constantly discredits it by crying up a rationalistic enlightenment. It would appear from this that his philosophical tact is somewhat feminine, and that, as intelligence, it does not exist. His poetic intelligence is of the finest: and if he doesn't know what liberty is, he understands poetry, and how to write it. This is enough for one man to know. And the thirty *Cantos* are enough to occupy a loving and ceaseless study—say a canto a year for thirty years, all thirty to be read every few weeks just for the tone.

IV. JOHN PEALE BISHOP

OF the American poets whose first books were published between 1918 and 1929 not more than six or seven are likely to keep their reputations until the end of the present decade. Eliot and Pound are pre-war. Crane, Marianne Moore, MacLeish, and Ransom are among the slightly more than half a dozen. The two or three other places may be disputed; but I take it that since 1929 there has been no new name unless it be that of a young man, James Agee, whose first volume appeared in 1934. John Peale Bishop, whose first poetry goes back to the war period but whose first book, *Now With His Love,* came out in 1932, will, I believe, rank among the best poets of the last decade.

His position has been anomalous. His contemporaries made their reputations in a congenial critical atmosphere, and they have been able to carry over a certain prestige into virtually a new age. (Ages crowd upon one another in a country that has never been young.) But Bishop has lacked that advantage. The first criticism accorded him was largely of the pinkish complexion. Mr. Horace Gregory, shrewdly discerning the poet's technical skill, became quickly concerned about the sincerity of a man who ignored the "class struggle." Bishop was not, in fact, asked whether he was a poet but whether he expected to survive capitalism: whether given his roots in the war-gen-

52

eration and the prejudices of the "ruling class," he could hope to achieve the portage over to the "main stream" of American letters recently discovered by Mr. Granville Hicks.

The problems of poetry must necessarily be the same in all ages, but no two ages come to the same solutions. Happiest is that age which, like the age of Sidney and Spenser, felt no need to reduce the problems to ultimate philosophical terms: our critical apparatus is immeasurably more thorough than theirs, our poetic performance appreciably worse. But our problems are inevitably theirs. They are the problem of language and the problem of form. The Elizabethan solution was practical, not speculative. The simple didacticism of the neo-classical Renaissance was as far as the sixteenth century got philosophically. The poets wrote better than they knew. Our knowledge is better than our performance.

In ages weak in form, such as our own age, theory will concentrate upon form, but practice upon the ultimate possibilities of language. Ages that create great varieties of forms, as the Elizabethans did in every branch of poetry, talk about language but actually take it for granted, and score their greatest triumphs with form. The powers of the language were not in the long run determined by theory, but instinctively by poets whose dominating passion was form: the language was determined by the demands of the subject. The more comprehensive the subject, the broader the symbolism, the more profoundly relevant the scheme of reference to the whole human experience, the richer the language became. The experiment with language as such is *The Shepherd's Calendar,* and it is a failure; but even there the poet attempts only to enlarge his vocabulary with archaic words for "poetical" effect. There is no trace of that forcing of language beyond its natural limits that we find in modern verse. Propriety of diction was the problem, and it was ably discussed by Puttenham in his long *Arte of English Poesie,* a work in every respect comparable to *The Principles of Literary Criticism* by Mr. I. A. Richards, who talks not about the propriety of language but about its ultimate meaning. He thus leaves behind him language as an instrument and, by going into the *kinds* of meaning, converts the discussion into the peculiarly modern problem of form. For form is meaning and nothing but meaning: scheme of reference, supporting symbolism that ceases to support as soon as it is recognized as merely that.

Metrics as a phase of the problem of form needs attention from modern critics. It is a subject poorly understood. It is usually treated as an air-tight compartment of technical speculation. Yet surely a metrical pattern is usable only so long as it is attached to some usable form. It is a curious fact that modern metrics reflects the uncertainty of modern poets in the realm of forms. So the modern poet, struggling to get hold of some kind of meaning, breaks his head against the *impasse* of form, and when he finds no usable form he finds that he has available no metrical system either. For those fixed and, to us, external properties of poetry, rhyme and metrical pattern, are, in the ages of their invention, indeed fixed but not in the least external. It is probable that there is an intimate relation between a generally accepted "picture of the world" and the general acceptance of a metrical system and its differentiations into patterns.

This is to say that the separate arts achieve their special formalisms out of a common center of experience. And from this center of experience, this reference of meaning, any single art will make differentiations within itself: epic, lyric, tragedy, comedy, each with its appropriate pattern of development. When the center of life disappears, the arts of poetry become the art of poetry. And in an advanced stage of the evil, in the nineteenth century and today, we get the *mélange des genres,* one art living off another, that the late Irving Babbitt so valiantly combated without having understood the influences that had brought it about. Painting tries to be music; poetry leans upon painting; all the arts "strive toward the condition of music"; till at last seeing the mathematical structure of music, the arts become geometrical and abstract, and destroy themselves.

The specialization of scientific techniques supplanting a central view of life has, as Mr. John Crowe Ransom showed in a recent essay,* tended to destroy the formal arts: poetry has in turn become a specialization of æsthetic effects without formal limitations. And, as Mr. Edmund Wilson has argued in *The Canons of Poetry,*† the

* *The Yale Review,* Spring, 1935; Vol. XXIV, no. 3; p. 501 ff.
† *The Atlantic Monthly,* April, 1934; Vol. 153, no. 4; pp. 455 ff.

novel now does the work formerly done by epic and tragedy, forms too "limited" and "artificial" for modern minds. The novel is the least formal of the literary arts; it rose, in fact, upon the débris of the *genres;* and it has been able to drive the formal literary arts from the public interest because, appealing to the ordinary sense of reality fostered by information, science, and journalism, the novelist neither sets forth symbolic fictions nor asks the reader to observe formal limitations.

The poet then at this time must ask, not what limitations he will be pleased, after the manner of the young Milton, to accept, but whether there are any that he can get. I assume that a poet is a man eager to come under the bondage of limitations if he can find them. As I understand John Peale Bishop's poetry, he is that eager man. It is a moral problem, but that phase I cannot touch here. Bishop has no settled metrics; but that too is an aspect of the formal problem that cannot be discussed in the limited space of a note.

It has been said that Bishop has imitated all the chief modern poets. He has virtually conducted his poetical education in public. But the observation is double-edged. In our age of personal expression the poet gets credit for what is "his own": the art is not the thing, but rather the information conveyed about a unique personality. Applauding a poet only for what is uniquely his own, we lose thereby much that is good. If a poem in Yeats' manner appears in Bishop's book, and is as good as Yeats', it is as good there as it is anywhere else.

56

More than most living poets Bishop has felt the lack of a central source of form. He is not the poet of personal moods and idle sensation. He constantly strives for formal structure. He has studied closely the poets of his time who, like Yeats, seem to have achieved, out of a kind of galvanized mythology or by means of a consciously restricted point of view, a working substitute for the supernatural myth and the concentration that myth makes possible. It is, I think, interesting to observe that in Bishop two contemporary influences, Yeats and Eliot, meet strongly, and meet only in him of all the contemporary poets whom I know anything about: Yeats for form, Eliot for the experiment in language. Only the best Yeats is better than this:

> And Mooch of the bull-red
> Hair who had so many dears
> Enjoyed to the core
> And Newlin who hadn't one
> To answer his shy desire
> Are blanketed in the mould
> Dead in the long war.
> And I who have most reason
> Remember them only when the sun
> Is at his dullest season.

It is not necessary to illustrate the early influence of Eliot, for it appears in *Now With His Love,* as the scholars say, *passim.* I will quote two poems that are harder to "place." To critics interested in poetry as private property it may be said that they are evidently his own. The poems—they must be read as carefully climaxed wholes—seem to me to be among the most successful in modern verse:

THE RETURN

Night and we heard heavy and cadenced hoofbeats
Of troops departing: the last cohorts left
By the North Gate. That night some listened late
Leaning their eyelids toward Septentrion.

Morning flared and the young tore down the trophies
And warring ornaments: arches were strong
And in the sun but stone; no longer conquests
Circled our columns; all our state was down

In fragments. In the dust, old men with tufted
Eyebrows whiter than sunbaked faces, gulped
As it fell. But they no more than we remembered
The old sea-fights, the soldiers' names and sculptors'.

We did not know the end was coming: nor why
It came; only that long before the end
Were many wanted to die. Then vultures starved
And sailed more slowly in the sky.

We still had taxes. Salt was high. The soldiers
Gone. Now there was much drinking and lewd
Houses all night loud with riot. But only
For a time. Soon the taverns had no roofs.

Strangely it was the young the almost boys
Who first abandoned hope; the old still lived
A little, at last a little lived in eyes.
It was the young whose child did not survive.

Some slept beneath the simulacra, until
The gods' faces froze. Then was fear.
Some had response in dreams, but morning restored
Interrogation. Then O then, O ruins!

Temples of Neptune invaded by the sea
And dolphins streaked like streams sportive
As sunlight rode and over the rushing floors
The sea unfurled and what was blue raced silver.

The poem avoids the difficulty of form by leaning upon a certain violence of language. The form of *The Return* is a very general idea about the fall of Rome. The implications of the form are not wide; and it is a typical modern form in that it offers a rough parallelism with the real subject—which in this poem is modern civilization—and not a direct approach to the subject. Where shall the poet get a form that will permit him to make direct, comprehensive statements about modern civilization? Doubtless nowhere. As a feat of historical insight the "form" of *The Return* is commonplace; yet the poem is distinguished. The poet has manipulated language into painting. The line "Temples of Neptune invaded by the sea" is by no means the same as its prose paraphrase: civilizations die of an excess of the quality that made them great; we, too, shall perish when we no longer have the temple of Neptune, the form, to preserve us from the limitless energy of the sea—that which the form held in leash. But "Rome" is here not a symbol of anything; our inferences about modern civilization are obvious, but they are not authorized by the poem. "The poem," writes Bishop, "is a simile in which one term of the comparison is omitted." It is rather that by means of a new grasp of language, very different from the mere "word-painting" of eighteenth-century nature poetry, the poet achieves a plastic objectivity that to some degree liberates him from the problem of finding a structural background of idea.

PERSPECTIVES ARE PRECIPICES

Sister Anne, Sister Anne,
Do you see anybody coming?

> I see a distance of black yews
> Long as the history of the Jews

> I see a road sunned with white sand
> Wide plains surrounding silence. And

> Far off, a broken colonnade
> That overthrows the sun in shade.

Sister Anne, Sister Anne,
Do you see nobody coming?

> A man
> Upon that road a man who goes
> Dragging a shadow by its toes.

> Diminishing he goes, head bare
> Of any covering even hair.

> A pitcher depending from one hand
> Goes mouth down. And dry is sand

Sister Anne, Sister Anne,
What do you see?

> His dwindling stride. And he seems blind
> Or worse to the prone man behind.

Sister Anne! Sister Anne!

> I see a road. Beyond nowhere
> Defined by cirrus and blue air.

I saw a man but he is gone
His shadow gone into the sun.

What I have said about *The Return* applies with even
greater force to *Perspectives Are Precipices*. This poem I
would cite as the perfect example of the effects of painting achieved in poetry. Criticism of this kind of poetry
must necessarily be tentative. Yet I think it is plain that
this particular poem has not only the immediate effect
of a modern abstract painting; it gives the complete illusion of perspective, of objects-in-the-round. Take the
"road sunned with white sand"—instead of "sunlight on
a sandy road," the normal word-structure for this image.
Even more striking is "Wide plains surrounding silence."
I leave it to the schoolmen, wherever they are, to decide
whether "silence" is commonly abstract or concrete; yet
it is certain that in Bishop's phrase it acquires a spatial,
indeed almost sensory, value that would have been sacri-
ficed had he written: "silence over the surrounding
plains."

It is worth remarking here that the line, "Long as the
history of the Jews," is the only clear example of "metaphysical wit" that I have been able to find in Bishop's
verse. It is possibly a direct adaptation of a passage from
Marvel:

And you should if you please refuse
Till the conversion of the Jews.

Bishop's line is the more striking for its isolation in his
work, but I think it is clearly a violation of the plastic

technique of the poem, and a minor blemish. The influence of Eliot, which could lead two ways, to the metaphysicals and to the symbolists, led Bishop almost exclusively to the latter. And he has perfected this kind of poetry in English perhaps more than any other writer.

It is an obscure subject: the Horatian formula *ut pictura poesis* bore fruit long before Heredia and Gautier—as early, in English verse, as Milton. But the mixtures of the *genres* acquired a new significance after the late nineteenth-century French poets began to push the borders of one sense over into another. It was not merely that the poet should be allowed to paint pictures with words— that much the Horatian phrase allowed. It was rather that the new "correspondences" among the five senses multiplied the senses and extended the medium of one art into the medium of another. Rimbaud's absurd sonnet on the colors of the vowels was the extreme statement of an experiment that achieved, in other poets and in Rimbaud's own *Bateau Ivre,* brilliant results. But the process cannot go on beyond our generation unless we are willing to accept the eventual destruction of the arts. There is no satisfactory substitute in poetry for the form-symbol.

It is on this dilemma of symbolic form or plastic form that Bishop is intelligent and instructive. He has recently written: "I am trying to make more and more *statements,* without giving up all that we have gained since Rimbaud." The difficulty could not be more neatly put. Two recent poems, *The Saints* and *Holy Nativity,** are the

* *Minute Particulars.* By John Peale Bishop. New York: Alcestis Press, 1936.

result of this effort. The statement is form, the fixed point of reference; "all that we have gained since Rimbaud" is the enrichment of language that we have gained to offset our weakness in form.

The new experiment of Bishop's is not complete. In *Holy Nativity* the attempt to use the Christian myth collapses with a final glance at anthropology:

> Eagle, swan or dove
> White bull or cloud . . .

His treatment of the supernatural, the attempt to replace our secular philosophy, in which he does not believe, with a vision of the divine, in which he tries to believe, is an instance of our modern unbelieving belief. We are so constituted as to see our experience in two ways. We are not so constituted as to see it two ways indefinitely without peril. Until we can see it in one way we shall not see it as a whole, and until we see it as a whole we shall not see it as poets. Every road is long, and all roads lead to the problem of form.

A NOTE ON DONNE

I

DONNE'S modern reputation has risen so suddenly
that writers born since 1900 may look back to the
time when he was a name in *The Oxford Book of English Verse* at the head of seven poems, two of which we
now know that he did not write. *A Garland for John
Donne*,* the collection of essays edited by Mr. Theodore
Spencer for the tercentenary of the poet's death, attempts
to revalue the poetry and to enquire into the causes of its
contemporary influence. The uncertainty of these critics
about Donne's place is remarkable in the case of a poet
three hundred years dead. The uncertainty comes of
Donne's being still alive. He "ranks" possibly a little
above Marvel, but Marvel's interest for us is not nearly so
great. The reasons for his influence are at once more difficult to discover and more fruitful to pursue than his
rank. The essayists in this volume are united in the belief
that many of Donne's problems are our own.

Johnson blamed the vices of metaphysical style upon "a
voluntary deviation from nature in pursuit of something
new and strange." The eighteenth century on the whole
regarded Donne as a prodigy of perverse learning. Although Donne's style, the bold images and learned conceits, had a distant effect upon Cowley and Carew, and

---

* *A Garland for John Donne, 1631–1931*, edited by Theodore Spencer.
Harvard University Press, 1932.

64

even Richard Crashaw; although the conversational tone influenced Dryden, it has remained for our own age to discover in him the main stream of English verse. It has been our task to understand the seriousness of the impulse and the integrity, which once seemed the perversity, of style; our task to see the whole intellectual structure of the poetry, along with the rough versification, in the light of the underlying problems of the age of Donne. For the first time he is being felt as a contemporary.

The eight essays are admirably distributed over the two kinds of problem that a great poet of the past inevitably creates—the historical and the critical problem. There are five historical essays. Mr. Spencer has written, in *Donne and His Age,* a study of the intellectual climate in which Donne lived: although he suggests more problems than he can solve in so brief a space, his discussion of the revolutionary effect of the sixteenth-century "picture of the physical world" on moral ideas is a valuable contribution to Elizabethan criticism. Mr. John Sparrow's *The Date of Donne's Travels* reviews difficult and perhaps insoluble problems of the poet's biography; incidentally Mr. Sparrow throws some light on the origin of Donne's geographical allusions—whether they were bookish or drawn from observation. *A Note on Donne the Preacher,* by Mr. John Hayward, presents a side of Donne that would have only a minor historical value had he never written his verse. Mrs. Evelyn M. Simpson's analysis of the *Paradoxes and Problems* brings out the early influence of Martial, an influence that Mr. Spencer finds general in the 1590's and not peculiar to Donne; Mrs. Simpson's paper is chiefly valuable for its emphasis on his early "interest in science."

But here, just as Mr. Eliot warns us that Donne's skepticism, being mainly an uncertainty about the right terms of faith, was not like ours, Mrs. Simpson might well have distinguished between science as we know it and Donne's "interest" in the new cosmologists, Copernicus and Kepler. This was rather an anxiety about the physical limits of consciousness and the bearing of that question on the scholastic conception of body and soul, which Donne presents in the terminology of St. Thomas. Donne knew nothing of a scientific age, or of the later, open conflict between the two world-views, science and religion. Far from having a scientific attitude towards the problem of body and soul, he grapples with it, not to get any truth out of it apart from his own personality, but to use it as the dramatic framework for his individual emotion.

This is the center of Donne. Mr. Mario Praz, in *Donne's Relation to the Poetry of His Time,* says: "Donne's technique stands in the same relation to the average technique of Renaissance poetry as that of baroque to that of Renaissance painting. His sole preoccupation is with the whole effect." And, involved in the whole effect, is the quality of experience known to modern criticism as "emotional tone," an implicit form that is functional to the precise rendition of the individual experience. "He was," writes Mr. Praz, "like a lawyer choosing the fittest arguments for the case in hand; not a searcher after a universally valid truth": the fittest images and tropes by which to set forth, not a truth, but a complete emotion. The terms are not the terms of objective truth, to which the individual experience is trimmed down, and all the implications rejected that the terms do not contain. They are rather occasional indications of an experience that is no longer implicit in them, to be used only when they serve the purpose. The scholastic terms in *The Extasie* associate democratically with the humble violet:

> But as all severall soules containe
>   Mixture of things, they know not what,
> Love, these mixt soules, doth mixe againe,
>   And makes both one, each this and that.
> A single violet transplant,
>   The strength, the colour, and the size . . .

The violet is no more purely illustrative than scholastic love; scholastic love occupies indifferent ground, with respect to truth, quite like that of the neutral conceit of the compasses in *A Valediction forbidding mourning:*

> If they be two, they are two so
>   As stiffe twin compasses are two,
> Thy soule the fixt foot, makes no show
>   To move, but doth, if the other doe.

The conceits in both passages are "neutral" because they may be either true or false with respect to the inherent demands of the emotion to be set forth in the poem.

This is the modernism of Donne: it is the modernism

that re-establishes our own roots in the age of Donne. Mr. Praz's essay is the link between the two problems of Donne—his place in his own time and his value for us. Here Mr. T. S. Eliot, prophesying the speedy decline of Donne's new reputation, leaves its future ominously obscure. Mr. Eliot's belief that Donne's prose—the sermons, *Biathanatos,* the *Paradoxes and Problems*—is ready for oblivion, and quickly, is not to be questioned; the sermons have been mildly popular, among those who wish to be in the Donne fashion without taking the trouble to read the verse. But that the *Songs and Sonets,* the *Elegies,* most of the *Satires* and the *Divine Poems,* will not continue to be read for an indefinite time is an opinion harder to maintain.

"His learning," says Mr. Eliot, "is just information suffused with emotion . . . rather a humorous shuffling of the pieces; and we are inclined to read our own more conscious awareness of the apparent unrelatedness of things into the mind of Donne."

How much longer this "unrelatedness of things" will continue to be the background of poetry; whether it is not by now an emotional convention out of which minor poetic heresies, like Imagism or the more recent Objectivism, will at intervals appear; whether the local excitement of sensation will indefinitely obscure the formal qualities of the Spenserian-Miltonic kind of verse—these are questions that Mr. Spencer's memorial volume asks, but wisely does not answer. The answers, perhaps, would contain the future of poetry.

II

Why we are concerned with the future of any art is a mystery that Donne and his contemporaries could not have understood. But the difference between Donne and our age is not, in this respect, a radical one, and there was a definite place in Mr. Spencer's book for an essay on the rise of the historical consciousness.

The position of Mr. George Williamson, in his excellent paper, *Donne and Today,* falls into two parts that tend to undermine each other. On the one hand, he suggests abstract analogies between Donne and some living poets, which would be interesting if true, but on the other hand, his quotations from Eliot, Read, Ransom, and the late Elinor Wylie offer as little evidence of the influence of Donne, as Mr. Williamson understands it, as one might derive from Tennyson. Mrs. Ramsay, in *Donne's Relation to Philosophy,* quotes stanzas from Donne and *In Memoriam* in order to distinguish two uses of "philosophy" in verse. But the lines of Tennyson come within Mr. Williamson's formula for Donne: "One may say that Donne's emotion is commonly given 'conceptual' form, but not that he is a philosophical poet."

Mr. Eliot remarks that Donne first made it possible to *think* in English lyrical verse; but it does not follow that his thinking in verse was our kind of thought. We are actually nearer to Tennyson. What thinking there is in modern verse has the general character of historical thinking—"And all the wars have dwindled since Troy fell." Tennyson innocently culled the scraps from the tables of "culture"; but our dietetics is more self-conscious. We use the past and we think about its meaning. Our framework of idea is the cultural cycle, or the awareness of the "pastness" of the past, as in the case of Mr. Archibald MacLeish. The vulgarity of the present and the purity of the past make the framework of Mr. John Crowe Ransom's irony. Even Mr. Jeffers performs a fusion of literary psychology with a fictitious primitivism that places him in the historical consciousness. Although Mr. Ezra Pound's method is a cunning imitation of the pre-historical view that seized past and present naïvely as a whole, the *Cantos* is a monument to the historical mentality. There is none of this explicitly in Donne.

There is, so far as I know, only the slightest evidence, in seventeenth-century poetry, of a sense of historical rise-and-fall affecting the moral temper of individuals. Milton's Latin poem, *Naturam non pati senium,* argues that nature does not inwardly decay. Civilization apart from nature is not mentioned; and the poem ends with an allusion to the Christian myth: *Ingentique rogo flagrabit machina mundi.* The decay of nature was a frequent subject of controversy in the universities, and Milton must have felt its latent hostility to his own settled belief in the relation between a fixed human nature and a perfect divine order.

It is this perfect divine order that makes Milton's mythology possible. It is the threat to such an order from the direction of the "new philosophy" which "calls all in doubt," the new cosmology, that compelled Donne to ignore the popular pastoral convention of his time; nor could he rest secure upon the more pretentious classical or Christian mythology. These imaginative structures (to describe them in the lowest terms) were by habit or in essence involved in the mediæval system. Mr. Williamson remarks: "Although mythology is banished from his verse, mediæval philosophy and Renaissance science take its place, in fact become his mythology." The distinction between abstract ideas and mythology is extremely important in the study of Donne, and I believe Mr. Williamson misses a capital point. Dante could afford to be philosophical; the terms were a system that he acknowledged as truth. But it is different with Donne; the vocabulary is merely vocabulary, and it lacks the ultimate, symbolic character of a myth. It is only a step from his lawyer-like use of ingenious terms to the intricacy of personal sensation as the center of consciousness. And from this it is but one more step, for the philosophical egoist, to the dramatization of oneself against the background of society or history. It is a step that Donne could not take, but doubtless would take were he alive today.

There was the mythological, pastoral school, begun by Wyat and Surrey, and Nicholas Grimald, improved by Sidney and Spenser, and perfected by Milton at a single stroke. There was the dramatic, introspective school which, whether in the lyric or on the stage, centered after Chapman in the individual sensibility. In the non-dramatic poets of this school, of whom Donne is the great figure before Dryden, the poet himself becomes the dramatic character: Mr. Spencer finds an analogy between Donne and Hamlet's philosophical egoism of inaction: the poet's ideas, now the framework of intense excitement, are pitted against one another like characters in a play.

Therein lies the nature of the "conceit." It is an idea not inherent in the subject, but exactly parallel to it, elaborated beyond the usual stretch of metaphor into a supporting structure for a long passage or even an entire poem. It may be torn away from its original meaning, like the Angels in Donne's *Elegie XI,* and yet remain the vehicle of "poetic truth"; that is to say, of heightened emotion in the poet's dramatization of his own personality. The conceit in itself is neither true nor false. From this practice it is but a step to Dryden and the eighteenth century, to the rise of the historical consciousness, and to ourselves. It is the peculiar fascination of Donne that he presents the problem of personal poetry in its simplest terms. There is the simple awareness, complicated at the surface by the immense resources of a gigantic mind, of frustration and bewilderment—to which, for us, is added the frustration of historical relativity. Milton stood for the historical absolute, which is the myth. And unless it will again be possible for men to give themselves up to a self-contained, objective system of truths, the principles of Donne, whether we know him or not, will continue to be our own.

A NOTE ON ELIZABETHAN SATIRE

I

AS the Oxford anthologies come off the press, the dis-
advantages of dividing English poetry into exact
centuries become more and more conspicuous. Sir Edmund Chambers, in his preface to *The Oxford Book of
Sixteenth Century Verse,* remarks that the year 1600 "still
finds a continuous flood of literature in mid-career." He
points out that "Drayton and Chapman, who hopelessly
overlap the dividing line, must be cut asunder." Drayton,
for example, suffers for the absence of his "ballads" of
Agincourt and the Virginian Voyage. Donne is wholly
omitted, for reasons that we shall see. Given the limited
range, which, in the poetry of Donne, Sir Edmund seems
to define with excessive narrowness, he has done his work
well, even brilliantly.

There is a good reason for the success of this anthology.
It is the editor's superior taste, a gift that historical scholars a generation ago feared to exercise. "In the present
case," writes Sir Edmund, "an attempt has been made to
apply a standard of absolute poetry, rather than one of
merely historical interest . . ." It is a difficult standard to
uphold, and if it cannot be said that the editor applies it
infallibly, that is because the power to perceive the best
does not always carry with it the will to reject the second
rate.

There are some minor disproportions in the representation of the poets. A debatable assumption underlies Sir Edmund's view of the whole period. The disproportion between Raleigh and Sir John Davies is enormous. Raleigh wrote less than Davies but that less is immeasurably superior; yet Davies has fifty-one pages to Raleigh's thirty-seven. Here one feels that Sir Edmund in spite of himself is beguiled by the historical interest of Davies' *Orchestra,* perhaps by the interminable facility of its versification—although Davies at times is still as clumsy as the earlier Gascoigne or Grimald.

One mark of Davies' inferiority is the lack of tension in his style, a lack of concentrated purpose. This inferiority is at the center of the whole Spenserian school, in which, as Sir Edmund points out, "the slightness of invention is overhung with ornamental decoration, like some great composition of Paolo Veronese...." This ornamental decoration of image in Spenser and Davies rose along with the historical improvement of English versification between 1557 and 1579—a springe to catch the woodcocks of the historical method. It was, actually, the resistance, in the first half of the century, of a fluid vocabulary to the poet's meaning, joined to his metrical uncertainty, that contributed to Wyat's success in "They flee from me that sometime did me seek." It is one of a half-dozen supremely great meditative lyrics in English.

Nevertheless, Sir Edmund justly attacks, from his own point of view, one of the hoariest pedantries in English criticism: "A rather irritating kind of scholarship insists

74

that Wyat was chiefly notable for the acclimatization of
the Italian sonnet. . . . But in lyric, sung or based on the
models of song, he is a master of the first order." . . . In
spite of the perhaps too generous excerpts from Davies,
Daniel and Constable, one sees everywhere the evidence
of Sir Edmund's preoccupation with the quality of the
verse. He has given us all of Sackville's *Induction;* six-
teen poems by Fulke Greville, including the fine long
piece, "Who grace for zenith had"; thirty-one pages of
Sidney, who is better represented here than in any other
popular collection ever made; and the ample selections
from Raleigh already noticed—although a few more of
his sonnets would have furthered the rising reputation of
this most neglected of Elizabeth's poets. Raleigh's direct,
conversational ease, his intelligence and subtlety, are
qualities that deserve to be better understood: it has been
the custom of a few centuries to see in Raleigh's verse
only a sort of thin lagging after Sidney. His poetry is, on
the contrary, distinct, and needs separate consideration.

II

It is ungrateful to impute to Sir Edmund Chambers any
trace of wrong insight into the quality of the age. The
century as a whole falls into three periods—that of Skel-
ton, lasting until the appearance of Wyat in Tottel's
Songes and Sonets in 1557; the period of Wyat, the most
considerable figure until Sidney and Spenser, whose
Shepherd's Calendar brought in a new era in 1579. It was

then the English Renaissance full-blown. *The Shepherd's Calendar,* a dull but original exercise in theory, offered to Spenser's successors an example of new possibilities of poetic English, and set up a pastoral convention that was to reach perfection as late as 1637. In singling out the leading impulse of the Elizabethan age one is constantly guided by the genius and magnitude of Spenser. Yet it is Milton in the next age who puts the seal of perfection on the pastoral, mythological school, and who, to no little extent, permits us to rank as highly as we do merely competent poets like Davies and Constable.

Our comparatively low rating of Greville no less than of Raleigh—Saintsbury says that Greville is "sententious and difficult"—is due to the constant introspection, the difficult self-analysis, the cynical melancholy, that break through the courtly pastoral convention to a level of feeling deeper, and historically purer, than the facile despair of the Sidneian sonneteers. Doubtless both Greville and Raleigh, as minor masters, were too much impressed with the glittering style of Sidney, and, later, of Spenser, to understand that their own sensibilities deserved a more perfectly matured style. Their work has the diffuseness of divided purpose.

There has never been enough made of Elizabethan satire. While Raleigh and Fulke Greville cannot be called pure satirists, they were not comfortable in the courtly, pastoral abstractions. In this negative feature of their verse they resemble certain of the satirists, Hall, Marston, Tourneur. If we put Raleigh and Greville together against the background of the widespread influence of Martial,* they, too, form a background not only to the *Satires* of Donne (1593) but to much of that great poet's most characteristic later writing.

Yet Sir Edmund says: "Only for chronology, indeed, can Donne be an Elizabethan"—an opinion that obscures the still powerful strain of mediæval thought at the end of the sixteenth century. By another kind of reasoning Donne cannot be a Jacobean. For we find in Donne, significantly enough, not only the influence of Martial, but a resurgence of scholasticism—a union of classical satire and mediævalism. And it is significant that "Go, soul, the body's guest" was written by the same Raleigh who wrote *The Passionate Man's Pilgrimage,* a poem that is, I believe, occasionally described as charming. I cannot believe that, in order to write it, Raleigh invoked a muse different from the muse of a poem that is sophisticated, consciously erudite, and subtle. *The Passionate Man's Pilgrimage* is mediæval allegory furbished up with a new awareness of the sensuous world; "Go, soul, the body's guest" is satire; and the two strains are not quite the disharmony that we are accustomed to believe them.

Possibly the last use of extended mediæval allegory in verse of great distinction is Sackville's *Induction.* There are the familiar personifications—Remorse, Dread, Revenge, Misery, Death. Spenser's task was to revive alle-

* See T. K. Whipple, *Martial and the English Epigram from Sir Thomas Wyat to Ben Jonson.* University of California Press, 1929; and Evelyn M. Simpson, *Paradoxes and Problems,* in *A Garland for John Donne.* Harvard University Press, 1931.

gory with a new spirit alien to the mediæval mind. Although Spenser's puritanism is manifest, his allegory has a voluptuous glitter that Sackville's more mediæval spareness lacked; or if you go back to Gower's treatment of the seven deadly sins it is plain that as a mediæval man he was too serious about them to dress them up.

The mediæval minds left over at the end of the sixteenth century tended to see the world not in terms of a fixed moral system, but with an ingrained moral prejudice about the nature of man. I allude here to the decline of Catholic theology in England, and to the rise, conspicuously in the dramatic poets, of an unmoral and antidoctrinal point of view. Marlowe is an example. But the moral temper of a less expansive, more melancholy age, a kind of interregnum between feudalism and Tudorism when the evil of life was expressed in ideas of all-pervasive mortality—this moral temper, having lost its theological framework, remained as an almost instinctive approach to the nature of man. And the nature of man, far from enjoying the easy conquest of evil that Spenser set forth in six books that might have been twelve, was on the whole unpleasant and depraved. This depravity is the theme of Elizabethan tragedy, I think, as early as *The Jew of Malta*. There is no need to cite Webster and Ford.

It is the prevailing attitude of the satirists and of most of those non-dramatic poets who stand apart from the Spenserian school. In such poets we find a quality that we have shortsightedly ascribed uniquely to modern verse —the analysis of emotion and an eye chiefly to the æsthetic effect. There is here the use of symbols that are too complex to retain, throughout a long work, or from one work to another, a fixed meaning. The allegorical symbol is constant and homogeneous, like the Red Cross Knight; the richer, poetic symbol, like Prospero, does not invite the oversimplification of certain of its qualities, but asks to be taken in all its manifold richness.

It is this stream of Elizabethan poetry that has never been properly evaluated. We tend to forget, in fixing the relation of the Shakespearean drama to its sources, and of its text to the texts of contemporaries, that Shakespeare stands outside the allegorical school. It is thus difficult for us to take a further step and to see that he was closely connected with a much less conspicuous type of poetry that had been only superficially affected by the Renaissance. This was the dormant mediæval which, even after the new language of Wyat, survived in Sackville's *Induction.*

In a later poet like Greene the new courtly conventions *are too weak to sustain his restless sensibility.* Although Greene never mastered a style, his great vitality of image and rhythm is largely due to a naïvely skeptical grasp of the conventions of Sidney and Spenser. He uses them without ever quite believing them: as in the verse of Raleigh the convention offers just enough resistance to expression to lend to the poetry tension and depth. Though Greene is imperfect, he has none of Daniel's complacently perfect dullness.

It is this resistance of the language to full expression,

the strain between images and rhythm, opposites "yoked by violence together" in varying degrees of violence, that gives to English lyrical verse its true genius. It is a genius that permitted Milton to bring to the pastoral style a richness and subtlety of effect that Spenser never achieved. It is that quality of English style which is superior to age and school. It was perfectly mastered as early as Wyat:

> It was no dream; I lay broad waking:
>   But all is turned, thorough my gentleness
> Into a strange fashion of forsaking;
>   And I have leave to go of her goodness,
>   And she also to use newfangleness.
>   But since that I so kindly am served
>   I would fain know what she hath deserved.

It is in the lyrics, even in the political satires, of Dryden, but it begins to disappear in Pope, to reappear in the nineteenth century perhaps in Landor and Browning alone. It is a quality, not of system or doctrine, but of immediate intelligence acting directly; a definite but unpremeditated limitation of moral and metaphysical idea to the problem of the work to be done. It is unmoralistic and anti-allegorical. Out of that long and neglected stream of the English tradition comes a type of poetry that we have named in modern times symbolism—a curious misnomer borrowed from the French; for it has no elaborate symbolism at all in the Spenserian mode.

When Saintsbury thirty-five years ago issued the first edition of his *Short History of English Literature*, he announced that his chief interest throughout would be form

—at that time a revolutionary point of view. But he gave
to the Elizabethan satirists only a scant paragraph: they
were both "coarse" and "insincere." This view will have
to be changed before we shall be able to understand the
early Donne—not only Donne, but a great deal of the
finest work of our own time, poets like Eliot and Yeats.
The satirists of the 1590's not only read Martial, they went
back through Sackville to Lyndsay and Dunbar. The mediæval sense of mortality, of the vanity of the world, survives in the satirists, who use it as a weapon of critical
irony upon the vaunting romanticism of the Renaissance.
And we, in this age, in so far as we maintain the traditions of English verse, are still criticizing the Renaissance.

III

The poetry of our own age that we find most moving
and powerful, the poetry that is tough enough to reject
the easy solutions of the human predicament that arise in
every age, has a longer and more honorable lineage than
we are accustomed to suppose. Yet Mr. Edmund Wilson,
in *Axel's Castle,* would have us believe that modern symbolism is a method, invented by the poets, of evading the
problems of modern economics: our belief in the inferiority of our own age to the past is due to the palsied irresponsibility of the Ivory Tower. But this belief is the fundamental groundwork of all poetry at all times. It is the
instinctive counter-attack of the intelligence against the
dogma of future perfection for persons and societies. It

is in this sense that poetry is most profoundly the criticism of life.

It must seem to readers who have preserved, in the midst of the historical method, a vestige of the historical sense, that social critics wish to exempt the world of secular policy from the criticism with which the arts are constantly threatening the latest programs of social improvement. It has always been so with the proponents of "proletarian" art; it was so with Spenser. The poets are asked to oversimplify the human predicament with morality and allegory. The first great example of proletarian—that is, allegorical—poetry in English is Spenser's *Faerie Queen:* there is no real distinction possible between an art that oversimplifies our experience in favor of princes and an art that performs that callow office for the people. There has always been a small body of men —a saving remnant very different from the Victorian notion of such a minority—headed by William Shakespeare, who warn us to make haste slowly with the best-wrought schemes for the satisfaction of our desires. Let the plans be well-wrought indeed, but let the arts teach us—if we demand a moral—that the plans are not and can never be absolutes. Poetry perhaps more than any other art tests with experience the illusions that our human predicament tempts us in our weakness to believe.

THREE TYPES OF POETRY

I

IN this essay I propose to discuss three kinds of poetry that bring to focus three attitudes of the modern world. I do not say all three attitudes, because there are more than three attitudes. And there are more than three kinds of poetry.

The first attitude is the spirit of the practical will: in poetry until the seventeenth century it leaned upon morality and allegory; now, under the influence of science, it has appealed to abstract ideas. It looks from explanation to action. The second attitude has been developed from the second phase of the first; it is a revolt against the domination of science; and in poetry it has given us the emotion known as "romantic irony." The third attitude is nameless because it is perfect, because it is complete and whole. Criticism may isolate the imperfect, and formulate that which is already abstract; but it cannot formulate the concrete whole. There is no philosophical or historical name for the kind of poetry that Shakespeare wrote. I shall call it, in this essay, the creative spirit. I use the term for convenience, and ask the reader to forget its current uses by the followers of the Expressionist school.

We happen to be dominated at the moment by the scientific spirit of the practical will. A hundred and fifty years ago rose the thin cry of romantic irony—the poet's self-pity upon the rack of science, which he mistook for reality. Most notably in the sixteenth century we had the creative spirit.

The reader is asked to keep in mind two general statements with some brief commentary:

First, the power of seizing the inward meaning of experience, the power of sheer creation that I shall call here the vision of the whole of life, is strictly *a quality of the imagination*. The apologists of science speak as if this were the scientific attitude, but the aim of science is to produce a mechanical whole for the service of the practical will. Our experience of a machine—even if our world were mechanical—is very different from our capacity to run it. For the imaginative whole of life is the wholeness of vision at a particular moment of experience; it yields us the quality of the experience.

It may be conveyed in a poem of four or six lines or in an epic of twelve books; or the twelve books may contain less of it than the four lines. Blake's *To the Accuser* is the total vision in eight lines; Darwin's *The Loves of the Plants* is the aimlessly statistical aggregation of fact—pseudo-botany or semi-science—in a number of lines that I have not counted.

Second, there is a surer grasp of the totality of experience in Wyat's *To His Lute* than in Shelley's *Adonäis*. This is the center of the problem of poetry. We must understand that the lines

> Life like a dome of many-colored glass
> Stains the white radiance of eternity

84

are not poetry; they express the frustrated individual will trying to compete with science. The will asserts a rhetorical proposition about the whole of life, but the imagination has not seized upon the materials of the poem and made them into a whole. Shelley's simile is imposed upon the material from above; it does not grow out of the material. It exists only as explanation external to the subject: it is an explanation of "life" that seems laden with portent and high significance, but *as explanation* it necessarily looks towards possible action, and it is there that we know that the statement is meaningless. Practical experimental knowledge can alone fit means to ends.

If the simile of the dome were an integral part of a genuine poem, the question of its specific merit as truth or falsehood would not arise. Yet Shelley's dome, as an explanation of experience, is quite as good as Edgar's reflection on his father's downfall:

Ripeness is all.

But the figure rises from the depth of Gloucester's situation. It is a summation not only of Gloucester's tragedy but of the complex tensions of the plot before the catastrophe in the last scene. Possibly the play would be as good without Edgar's words; but it is significant that we cannot imagine the play without the passage ending in those words. They are absolutely implicit in the total structure, the concrete quality, of the whole experience that we have when we read *King Lear*. The specific merit of Edgar's statement as general truth or falsehood is irrelevant because it is an *experienced statement*, first from Edgar's, then from our own, point of view; and a statement remains experienced, and thus significant and comprehensible, whether it be true or false.

The truth or falsity of Shelley's figure is the only issue that it raises. The idea must be accepted before we can accept the material of the poem *Adonaïs;* for it must be a true idea to afford to the poet a true explanation. He must have an explanation for a material that he cannot experience. The idea of the dome is asserted to strengthen a subject that the poet has not implicitly imagined.

It was this quality of modern poetry that Arnold had in mind, or doubtless should have had in mind, when he remarked that the romantics "did not know enough." We have not known enough since their time. Arnold wrote later that the Victorian critics permitted the poet "to leave poetic sense ungratified, provided that he gratifies their rhetorical sense and their curiosity." If the term rhetoric must have an invidious meaning, I think we may understand Arnold somewhat in this manner: that rhetoric is a forcing of the subject, which is abstractly conceived, not implicitly seized upon. It is external and decorative in the early romantics of the mid-eighteenth century; it is hysterical, and evasive of the material, in the great romantics—and it excites the "curiosity" of the reader, who dwells on the external details of the poem or pities the sad poet. The reader is not given an integral work of art. How could criticism since Shelley and Wordsworth be anything but personal?—strive for anything but evaluation of personality? It has been given little else to evaluate. And why should not criticism fail in evaluating Shakespeare's personality? And is this not the glory of Shakespeare?

The reader's curiosity is motivated by his will. In the lowest terms, he seeks information (even from a poet); then, more purposefully, he seeks for the information an explanation that, if it is good, is some branch of science. But like the late Humanists he tries to get explanations from the poets.

"For what is rhetoric," wrote W. B. Yeats nearly thirty years ago, "but the will trying to do the work of the imagination?" Mr. Yeats, with insight as profound as it is unique in our time, has gone straight to the problem. Rhetoric is the pseudo-explanation of unimagined material. The "right" explanation—the exhibit of workable relations among different parts of any material—although always provisional, is the scientific explanation. When the will tries to do the work of the imagination, it fails, and only succeeds in doing badly the work of science. When the will supplants the imagination in poetry, the task of the poet, because his instrument is not adequate to his real purpose, which is that of explanatory science, is bound to be frustrated. We get the peculiar frustration of the poet known as romantic irony.

The pure scientific spirit I shall call here without much regard for accuracy, a positive Platonism, a cheerful confidence in the limitless power of man to impose practical abstractions upon his experience. Romantic irony is a negative Platonism, a self-pitying disillusionment with the positive optimism of the other program: the romantic tries to build up a set of fictitious "explanations," by means of rhetoric, more congenial to his unscientific temper. The creative spirit occupies an aloof middle ground —it is in no sense a compromise, as the late Irving Babbitt conceived it to be—between these positions. Its function is the quality of experience, the total revelation— not explanation for the purpose of external control by the will.

II

Dante distinguished two kinds of allegory. Religious allegory is both literally and figuratively true: we are to believe that the events of the story happened. But poetical allegory is true only in the figurative sense. The derivative meanings, called by Dante the moral and the anagogical, are legitimate, indeed they are the highest meanings; but they lean upon no basis of fact. Although fictional allegory is not popular today, it is the only sort that we can conceive. When the mediæval allegorist used the Bible, it never entered his head that he was not using historical fact; and he brought the same mentality to bear upon material that even we, who are sophisticated, recognize as historical.

But a modern poet, attempting allegory, undoes the history. We accept his figures and images as amiable make-believe, knowing that historical fact and poetic figure have no real connection, simply because there is nothing true but fact. About this fact science alone can instruct us, not with a fundamentally different kind of instruction from that of the allegorist, but with the same kind, more systematic and efficient. When the author of the popular poem, *John Brown's Body,* shows us the machine age growing out of Brown's body, we know that nothing of the sort happened, and we ask for the more enlightened view of the facts available in the scientific historians.

It is the kind of poetry that is primarily allegorical that seems to me to be inferior. It is inferior as science, and it is inferior as poetry. Mere allegory is a vague and futile kind of science. And because its primary direction is towards that oversimplification of life which is the mark of the scientific will, it is a one-sided poetry, ignoring the whole vision of experience. Although *The Divine Comedy* is allegorical, I think if it were mainly so it would not be one of the great poems of all time. It came out of an age whose mentality held the allegorical view of experience as easily as we hold the causal and scientific; so, in Dante, allegory never rises to an insubordinate place, but consistently occupies an implicit place, from which we must derive it by main force.

There is a general sense in which all literature may be apprehended as allegory, and that sense explains the popular level of literary appreciation. When certain moral ideas preponderate over others in any kind of literature, the crudely practical reader abstracts them, and contents himself with the illusion that they are the total meaning of the work. The naïve Roman Catholic may see only this phase of Dante, who for him might as well have written a tract. Now when the preponderance of meanings receives from the author himself the seal of his explicit approval, in face of the immense complication of our experience, then the work tends towards allegory. The work is written in the interest of social, moral, and religious ideas apart from which it has neither existence nor significance. And it is æsthetic creation at a low level of intensity. If the intention is innocent, the result is didacticism. If it is deliberate and systematic, and calculated to move people into some definite course of action, we get what is called in our time propaganda.

Didactic and propagandist works frequently have great artistic merit and power. Fiction different as *The Pilgrim's Progress* and *An American Tragedy* is overwhelming evidence of this. The perception of merit in this kind of writing has become a pretext, in our age, for believing that its defects, chiefly the defect of "propaganda," are a primary motive of all literature whatsoever. When the deficiency or impurity of inspiration is not forthright, it is nevertheless assumed as present but concealed: this is the kind of propaganda that is supposedly written from the security of a ruling class.

Pure allegory differs from this kind of writing in that the preponderance of meaning is wholly revealed; the characters, images, symbols, ideas, are simple, and invite restatement in a paraphrase that exhausts their meaning;

they stand, not in themselves, but merely for something else. *The Faerie Queene* belongs to this class of allegory. The summary remarks that I shall make about that great poem by no means encompass it; there is more to say that would not be to my purpose.

The structural feature that first impresses the reader of the poem is the arbitrary length of each canto: there is no reason inherent in the narrative why a canto should not be longer or shorter than it is. The characters in the story remain homogeneous throughout; that is to say, they suffer no dramatic alteration; an episode ends when they have acted out enough of the moral to please the poet. The action has no meaning apart from the preconceived abstractions, which we may call Renaissance Platonism or any other suitable name, so long as we remember that the ideas suffer no shock and receive no complication in contact with the narrative. The narrative lacks inner necessity; it is pure illustration. The capacity of the poet to allegorize the "philosophy" was illimitable, and terminated only with his death, which prevented completion of the poem.

One must remember that this sort of allegory has predominated in our tradition. Anglo-American literature, with the possible exception, at his high moments, of Nathaniel Hawthorne, has not given us allegory of the Dantesque order. I allude here not to Dante's style, but to his ability to look into a specific experience and to recreate it in such a way that its meaning is nowhere distinct from its specific quality. The allegorical interpretation is secondary. We get a genuine creation of the imagination. We get, in the Spenserian allegory, a projection of the will.

The quality and intention of the allegorical will are the intention and quality of the will of science. With allegory the image is not a complete, qualitative whole; it is an abstraction calculated to force the situation upon which it is imposed toward a single direction. In the sixteenth century science proper had achieved none of its triumphs. The allegorist had before him no standard by which he could measure the extent of his failure to find the right abstractions for the control of nature. He could spin out his tales endlessly in serene confidence of their "truth." But by the end of the eighteenth century his own optimism had waned; it had passed to the more efficient allegorist of nature, the modern scientist.

Now in a poet like Dante we may say that there is an element of "science" in so far as the allegorical interpretation is possible: *The Divine Comedy* has something to say, not only to our naïve Roman Catholic, but to the ordinary man whose prepossessions are practical, and whose literary appreciation is limited by the needs of his own will. The poem has a moral, a set of derivative ideas that seem to the reader to be relevant to practical conduct. But to say this is not to say, with most schools of modern criticism, that it is the primary significance of the work. For Dante is a poet; the didactic element is in solution with the other elements, and may be said barely to exist in itself, since it must be isolated by the violence of the reader's own will.

There is therefore a distinction to be drawn between a kind of writing in which allegorical meanings, if they are really present, are fused with the material, and pure and explicit allegory. It is the difference between works of the creative imagination and the inferior works of the practical will. The reader will recall my first proposition: the power of creating the inner meaning of experience is strictly a quality of the imagination. It is not a construction of the will, that perpetual modernism through which, however vast may be the physical extent of the poet's range, the poet ignores the whole of experience for some special interest. This modern literature of Platonism—a descriptive term used to set apart a kind of work in which the meanings are forced—carries with it its own critical apparatus. It is known at present as the revolutionary or social point of view. Since the rise of science it has been also the "capitalist" point of view. For our whole culture seems to be obsessed by a kind of literature that is derivative of the allegorical mentality.

By the time of Dryden allegory of the mediæval variety had lost its prestige; we get the political fables of *The Hind and the Panther,* of *Absalom and Achitaphel,* where the intention is pleasantly fictitious and local, with no pretense of universal truth. By the end of the next century the Platonic conquest of the world, the confident assertion of control over the forces of nature, had contrived a system of abstractions exact enough to assume the new name of science. So, in poetry, the allegorical mentality, which had hitherto used all the crude science available, lost confidence in its unexperimental ideas. The poetical assertion of the will took the form of revolt from its more successful counterpart, science. We find here two assertions of the same erring will, diverging for the first time: science *versus* romanticism.

III

With the decline then of mere allegory, we see the rise of a new systematic structure of entities called science, which makes good the primitive allegorist's futile claim to the control of nature. Between allegorist and scientist there exists the illusion of fundamental opposition. They are, however, of one origin and purpose.* For the apparent hostility of science to the allegorical entities is old age's preoccupation with the follies of its youth.

When this situation became fully developed, the poets, deprived of their historic fictions, and stripped of the means of affirming the will allegorically, proceeded to revolt, pitting the individual will against all forms of order, under the illusion that all order is scientific order. The order of the imagination disappeared. Thus arose romanticism, not qualitatively different from the naturalism that it attacked, but identical with it, and committed in the arts to the same imperfect inspiration.

* "Always science has grown up on religion . . . and always it signifies nothing more or less than an abstract melioration of these doctrines, considered as false because less abstract." Spengler: *The Decline of the West.*

This summary will, I believe, be illuminated by a passage from Taine, who is discussing Byron:

Such are the sentiments wherewith he surveyed nature and history, not to comprehend them and forget himself before them, but to seek in them and impress upon them the image of his own passions. He does not leave the objects to speak for themselves, but forces them to answer him.

We have the endless quest of the romantic, who ranges over nature in the effort to impose his volitional ego as an absolute upon the world. Compare Taine's analysis of Byron with a sentence from Schopenhauer:

While science, following the unresting and inconstant stream of the fourfold forms of reason and consequent, with each end attained sees further, and can never reach a final goal nor attain full satisfaction any more than by running we can reach the place where the clouds touch the horizon; art, on the contrary, is everywhere at its goal.

For the will of science and the will of the romantic poet (the frustrated allegorist) are the same will. Romanticism is science without the systematic method of asserting the will. Because it cannot participate in the infinite series of natural conquests, the romantic spirit impresses upon nature the image of its own passions:

Make me thy lyre, even as the forest is:
What if my leaves are falling like its own!
The tumult of thy mighty harmonies

Will take from both a deep autumnal tone,
Sweet though in sadness. Be thou, Spirit fierce,
My spirit! Be thou me, impetuous one!

It is the "will trying to do the work of the imagination." The style is inflated and emotive, without definable objective. The poet, instead of fixing his attention upon a single experience, instead of presenting objectively the plight of human weakness—the subject of his poem— flies from his situation into a rhetorical escape that gives his will the illusion of power. (It may be observed that at the culmination of French romanticism in Rimbaud, the poet, still caught upon the dilemma of the will, carried this dilemma to its logical and most profound conclusion —the destruction of the will.)

The momentary illusion of individual power is a prime quality of the romantic movement. In the intervals when the illusion cannot be maintained, arise those moments of irony that create the dramatic conflict of romantic poetry. In generalizing about such a quality one must take care; it differs with different poets. I have just pointed out incidentally how the individual will receives, in a late, and perhaps the greatest romantic, a self-destructive motivation. Yet the dramatic effect is similar in poets as different as Rimbaud and Shelley. Throughout the nineteenth century, and in a few poets today, we get an intellectual situation like this: there is the assumption that Truth is indifferent or hostile to the desires of men; that these desires were formerly nurtured on legend, myth, all kinds of insufficient experiment; that, Truth being known at last in the form of experimental science, it is intellectually impossible to maintain illusion any longer, at the same time that it is morally impossible to assimilate Truth.

The poet revolts from Truth; that is, he defies the cruel and naturalistic world to break him if it can; and he is broken. This moral situation, transferred to the plane of drama or the lyric, becomes romantic irony:

> I fall upon the thorns of life! I bleed!

His will being frustrated by inhospitable Truth, Shelley is broken; falls into disillusionment; and asks the west wind to take him away and make him its lyre. In a contemporary poet, whose death two years ago was probably the climax of the romantic movement in this country, we get precisely the same quality of irony. Invoking a symbol of primitive simplicity, Pocahontas, Crane says:

> Lie to us! Dance us back our tribal morn!

The poet confesses that he has no access to a means of satisfying his will, or to a kind of vision where the terms are not set by the demands of the practical will. He returns to a fictitious past. There he is able to maintain, for a moment, the illusion that he might realize the assertion of his will in a primitive world where Truth is not a fatal obstacle.

At this point we must notice a special property of the romantic imagination. It has no insight into the total meanings of actual moral situations; it is concerned with fictitious alternatives to them, because they themselves invariably mean frustration of the will. This special property of escape is the Golden Age, used in a special fashion. The romantic poet attributes to it a physical reality somewhere in space and time. In a great poet like Shakespeare, notably in *The Tempest,* we get the implications of the poetic convention of the Golden Age; properly looked at, it is more than a poetic convention, it is a moral necessity of man. The use to which Shakespeare puts it is not involved with the needs of his personal will; it assists in defining the quality of his insight into the ineradicable flaws of human character. For the Golden Age is not a moral or social possibility; it is a way of understanding the problem of evil, being a picture of human nature with the problem removed. It is a qualitative fiction, not a material world, that permits the true imagination to recognize evil for what it is.

Now the romantic and allegorical poet, once he is torn with disbelief in the adequacy of the poetic will, sees before him two alternatives. After falling upon the thorns of life, he may either ask the west wind to take him up, or cry for his tribal morn in the Golden Age: this is the first alternative—disillusionment with life after defeat of the will. He will seize this escape provided that he lacks the hardihood of a Rimbaud, who saw that, given the satisfaction of will as a necessity of the age, the poet must either destroy his will or repudiate poetry for a career of action. But Rimbaud is the exceptional, because he is the perfect, romantic poet.

The other ordinary alternative of the modern allegorist lies in the main Spenserian tradition of ingenuous tale-telling; it is the pure Golden Age of the future, which the poet can envisage with complacency because his will has not gone off into the frustration of romantic irony. He partakes of the efficient optimism of science; he asks us to believe that a rearrangement of the external relations of man will not alone make him a little more comfortable, but will remove the whole difficulty of evil, ushering in perfection. It is this type of crude, physical imagination that we find in a Victorian like Tennyson:

Till the war-drums sound no longer, and the battleflags are furled
In the Parliament of Man, the Federation of the World.

The cult of the will is a specially European or Western cult; it rose after the Middle Ages; and it informs our criticism of society and the arts. For, given the assumption that poetry is only another kind of volition, less efficient than science, it is easy to believe in the superiority of the scientific method. I myself believe in it. For the physical imagination of science is, step by step, perfect, and knows no limit. The physical imagination of poetry, granting it an unlimited range, is necessarily compacted of futile and incredible fictions, which we summarily reject as inferior instruments of the will. And rightly reject, if we assume two things—and our age is convinced that it is impossible to assume anything else: (1) that the only kind of imagination is that of the will, which best realizes its purposes in external constructions or in the control of the external relations of persons and things; (2) that this sole type of imagination will be disillusioned or optimistic, according as it is either imperfectly informed, as in mere poetry, or adequately equipped by science with the "fourfold forms of reason and consequent." That is the view held by a vociferous school of critics in this country, the most influential of whom has been Mr. Edmund Wilson in *Axel's Castle*, a book written on the assumption that *all* poetry is only an inferior kind of social will.

The critical movement so ably represented by Mr. Wilson is the heresy that I am opposing throughout this essay. That the kind of imaginative literature demanded by this school is the third, and I think necessarily the final, stage in the history of allegory in Western culture, may not be immediately clear.

The school preoccupied with what is called the economic determinism of literature is in the direct line of descent from the crudely moralistic allegory of the Renaissance. The notion that all art is primarily an apology for institutions and classes, though it is now the weapon of the Marxists against "capitalist" literature, has been explicit in our intellectual outlook since the time of Buckle in England, and Taine and Michelet in France. It is an article of faith in the "capitalist" and utilitarian dogma that literature, like everything else, must be primarily, and thus solely, an expression of the will. From such allegory as:

> With him went Danger, clothed in ragged weeds,
>   Made of bear's skin, that him more dreadful made,
> Yet his own face was dreadful, ne did need
>   Strange horror, to deform his grisly shade;
>   A net in th' one hand, and a rusty blade
> In th' other was, this Mischief, that Mishap . . .

—from this it is only a step to the sophisticated entities and abstractions of the agitation for social reform, whose vocabulary is an imitation, and an application to conduct, of the terms of physical science. Or rather, I should say, two steps; for the intermediate stage of allegory is the romantic irony of the age of Byron and Shelley. The contemporary allegorists have regained something of the easy confidence of their early forerunners; they believe as fully in the positive efficacy of the Marxian dialectic, as Spenser in the negative example of the Seven Deadly Sins.

Yet, the Seven Deadly Sins being now a little threadbare, our new allegorists are quite clear in their recognition that the arts, more especially poetry, have no specific function in society. The arts offer to society a most pusillanimous instrument for the realization of its will. The better the art, one must add, the more pusillanimous. For art aims at nothing outside itself, and, in the words of Schopenhauer, "is everywhere at its goal." There is no goal for the literature of the will, whose new objective must be constantly redefined in terms of the technology, verbal or mechanical, available at the moment.

The significance of this movement in modern society is perfectly plain: by seizing exclusively those aspects of the total experience that are capable of being put to predictable and successful use, the modern spirit has committed itself to the most dangerous program in Western history. It has committed itself exclusively to this program. We should do well to consider a specimen of contemporary romantic irony; the "He" in the passage is the Devil:

> He leaned his elbows on two mountain tops
> And moved his head slowly from side to side,
> Sweeping the plain with his unhurried eyes.
> He was the phoenix of familiar men,
> Of husbands I have known, the horns and all,
> But more, much more—O God, I was afraid.
> I would have hid before the eyes had come.
> Then they were there, and then
> My guts grew warm again in my despair
> And I cried "Pour la Reine" and drew my sword.
> But, Christ, I had no sword.

He had no science; the fictitious sword of the allegorical will that the hero "drew" was incompetent to deal with his desperately practical situation. Our new scientific allegorists rest their case against poetry there. What they neglect to provide for is the hero's failure in case he has a genuine sword of science. For the recognition of that other half of experience, the realm of immitigable evil— or perhaps I had better say in modern abstraction, the margin of error in social calculation—has been steadily lost. The fusion of human success and human error in a vision of the whole of life, *the vision itself being its own goal,* has almost disappeared from the world of the spirit.

IV

I have set forth two propositions about poetry. I will now ask the reader to examine a little more narrowly the second, in the attempt to discriminate between a poetry of the will and a poetry of genuine imagination. We have seen that the poetry of the will takes two forms. There is the romantic, disillusioned irony of Shelley, or for that matter of a poet like Mr. Robinson Jeffers; there is the crude optimism of a Victorian like Tennyson, a moral outlook that has almost vanished from poetry,* surviving today as direct political and social propaganda supported by the sciences. My second proposition was a brief commentary on the lines by Shelley:

> Life like a dome of many-colored glass
> Stains the white radiance of eternity.

The will asserts a general proposition about the whole of life, but there is no specific, imagined context to support the assertion. As a product of the imagination the passage is incomprehensible; as a practical, that is to say, as a scientific generalization, it is open to the just contempt of the scientific mind. What, then, is the exact purpose and function of such poetry?

In purpose it competes with science; as to function it has, quite simply, none. It is an affirmation of the will in terms that are not a legitimate vehicle of the will. The proper mode of the will—proper, that is, in efficiency, but not necessarily in morals, for the question whether the will should be so expressed at all is a distinct problem— the right mode of the will is some kind of practical effort adequately informed by exact science.

Most modern schools of criticism assume that all poetry is qualitatively the same as the lines by Shelley; they as-

---

* I make exception for Mr. Stephen Spender, the English poet.

sume this negatively, for the positive assumption is that poetry must of necessity be like science, a quantitative instrument for mastery of the world. This is the interesting theory of Mr. I. A. Richards: because poetry is compacted of "pseudo-statements" it cannot compete with "certified scientific statements," and must be discredited as science moves on to fresh triumphs. This point of view is doubtless inevitable in a scientific age; but it is not an inevitable point of view.

Mr. Richards' theory of the relation between poetry and our beliefs about the world appears novel to some critics. It is the latest version of the allegorical, puritan and utilitarian theory of the arts—a theory that is rendered, by Mr. Richards, the more plausible because it seems to give to the arts a very serious attention. The British utilitarians, a century ago, frankly condemned them. So, with less candor, does Mr. Richards: his desperate efforts to make poetry, after all, useful, consist in justly reducing its "explanation" to nonsense, and salvaging from the wreck a mysterious agency for "ordering our minds." Poetry is a storehouse of ordered emotional energy that properly released might re-educate the public in the principles of the good life. For brevity, I paraphrase Mr. Richards; it should be observed that the idea is set forth in terms of the will.*

Yet there is, even according to Mr. Richards, little hope for this kind of education. The "certified scientific statements" about the world make the metaphors, the images,

---

* My discussion is based upon Mr. Richards' two principal books: *The Principles of Literary Criticism*, 1924, and *Practical Criticism*, 1929.

the symbols, all the varieties of "pseudo-statements"—
similes like the dome of many-colored glass—look extremely foolish, because in the exacter light of science,
they are patently untrue. I do not intend here to discuss
this theory as a whole, nor to do justice to Mr. Richards'
poetic taste, which is superior. One part of the theory, I
believe, may be dismissed at once. How can poetry, a
tissue of lies, equip the public with "relevant responses"
to an environment? Our responses must work; they must
be, in at least a provisional sense, scientifically true. What
is this mysterious emotional function of poetry that orders our minds with falsehood?

Mr. Richards is, I believe, talking about the unstable
fringe of emotion that I have called romantic irony: we
have seen that this is what is left to the poet—a lugubri-
ous residue—after he realizes that science is truth and
that his own fictions are lies. This residue organizes and
orders nothing whatever. Mr. Richards' underlying assumption about poetry is, like Mr. Edmund Wilson's,
embedded in the humanitarian mentality of the age,
where it lies too deep for examination.

If the pseudo-statement is motivated by the will (the
only intention for it that Mr. Richards can conceive), it is
false, and Mr. Richards is right: the poet of this sort expects potatoes to grow better when planted in the dark
of the moon.

If, on the other hand, a genuine poet uses the pseudo-
statement, it is neither true nor false, but is a quality of
the total created object: the poem. The power to perceive

this total quality has almost disappeared from modern criticism. For all the arts are assumed to be necessarily assertions of the will.

Mr. Richards, like the romantic poet of the age of Byron and Shelley, sees that science has contrived a superior instrument of the will; again like them, he tries to rescue poetry by attributing to it functions of practical volition, functions that he cannot define but which, in the true liberal tradition, he asserts in some realm of private hope against the "truths" of science.

Now it seems to me that the foundations of poetry, and possibly of the other creative arts, are somewhat different. We cannot understand them until we shall have eliminated from our thinking the demands of the category of will with its instrument, the practical intellect.

Let us look at Mr. Richards' famous terms: "certified scientific statement" (science) and "pseudo-statement" (poetry). I will try to show briefly that, for poetry, the certified scientific statement is the half-statement. The pseudo-statement may be, as I have just said, neither true nor false, but a feature of the total quality of the poem. The lines

> Out, out brief candle!
> Life's but a walking shadow; a poor player
> That struts and frets his hour upon the stage,
> And then is heard no more . . .

are certainly not "true": we know that life is not a shadow, it is a vast realm of biological phenomena; nor is it a player. Neither are the lines false: they represent a stage in the dynamic unfolding of Macbeth's character, the whole created image of which is the whole play *Macbeth,* which in its turn is neither true nor false, but *exists as a created object.* None of the pseudo-statements in the play, representing the conflict of will that forms the plot, is either approved or disapproved by the poet. He neither offers us a practical formula for action nor rejects any of the volitional purposes of the characters. He creates the total object of which the pseudo-statements of the will are a single feature, and are therefore neither true nor false. What Mr. Richards' theory (and others like it) comes down to is the uneasy consciousness that such a passage as I have just quoted does not tell us how to keep out of the sort of mess that Macbeth got himself into. The ideal connection of this theory with the traditions of moralistic allegory is quite evident.

Before we may see the certified scientific statement as the half-statement, a further point of Mr. Richards' theory must be noticed. Poets, being ignorant of science and their general ideas false, ought to write poems in which appear no beliefs whatever, but in which, presumably, there is that mysterious ordering of our minds. *The Waste Land* is such a poem—supposedly. But is it? According to the poet himself and to my own simple powers of inspection, it is full of beliefs. Mr. Richards, with admirable aplomb, has seized upon a poem in which large generalizations do not appear, as an instance of his theory: that poets, to keep our respect, must order our minds without lies; that, in order to avoid saying wrong things, they must say nothing. And this "nothing" is only another species of half-statement. It leads straight to a defense of the recent school of "pure poets" in France,* a school that had its meeker followers in England and this country.

This half-statement may be in the pure poets an immersion in the supposedly pure sensations of experience.† But in the older romantics of the nineteenth century, it is due to a sentimental escape from the abstractions of science. And indeed both fallacies are due to a misunderstanding of the exact nature of the "certified scientific statement." We saw, in the second section of this essay, how the romantics revolted from science, or one kind of half-statement, giving us romantic irony. This irony has dwindled, in our day, to the other half-statement (to the other activity of the same will) of "pure poetry." It is significant that at the present time we get, from both scientist and pure poet, a renunciation of poetry because it cannot compete with the current version of our objective world, a version that is pre-empted by the demands of the will with its certified scientific statements.

It must be remembered that this kind of statement is invariably, and on principle, the half-statement. It is the statement about a thing, a person, an experience, which relates it to something else, not for the purpose of giving us intensive knowledge of the thing, person, or experience, in itself and as a whole; but simply to give us, in

* See *La Poesie Pure.* By Henri Bremond. Paris, 1926.
† Cp. R. P. Blackmur, who shows that E. E. Cummings' effort to achieve pure sensation ends in an "idea of sensation," an abstraction; in my terms, the half-statement. See note, p. 197.

varying degrees depending upon the exactness of the science under which it is viewed, the half-knowledge that limits us to the control of its extensive relations. If I feed a horse corn every day at noon, I may expect him to do more work in the afternoon than he would do without it. I am controlling the relation between grain and horse under the general proposition: Regular feeding of grain increases an animal's capacity to work. The statement must be either true or false.

But the statements in a genuine work of art are neither "certified" nor "pseudo-"; the creative intention removes them from the domain of practicality. "In æsthetics," wrote Mr. Leo Stein a few years ago in an excellent book, "we have to do with complex wholes which are never in a rigid state of adjustment."* This integral character of the work of art forever resists practical formulation. The æsthetic whole invites indefinitely prolonged appreciation; whereas the half-statement of science arrests our attention at those features of the whole that may be put to the service of the will. In the following verses the horse cannot be *used,* but as an object arousing prolonged contemplation in its particular setting it may be *known:*

> I set her on my pacing steed,
> And nothing else saw all day long,
> For sidelong she would bend, and sing
> A faëry's song.

The stanza is neither true nor false; it is an object that exists.

* *The ABC of Æsthetics.* By Leo Stein. New York, 1927.

I think it ought to be clear by this time that theories like Mr. Richards', theories covertly or avowedly concocted in the interest of social schemes, are not guides to the study of the immense qualitative whole of works of art; they are scientific (more or less) charts, relating the art-object to other objects at the behest of the practical will. So it may be said that such theories belong to that perpetually modern impulse to *allegorize* poetry, to abstract for use those features that are available for immediate action, and to repudiate the rest.

It ought to be clear that this is the regular course of science in the whole universe of objects; that with the arts science proceeds consistently, on principle; that society has developed an instinctive approach to the arts appropriate to the scientific temper of the age.

A man lives in a beautiful house in a beautiful place. Let him discover oil under his land. The oil has been there all the time as a feature of the total scene. But he violates the integrity of the scene by "developing" the oil. Where the house and land had previously existed for his loving contemplation, he abstracts one feature of it for immediate use under the ægis of Mr. Richards' certified scientific half-statements; and destroys its wholeness. Perhaps he was a dreaming kind of man: suppose he had always meant to get out the oil, and had gone about it with an improper method. Suppose that all he could do was to write a poem, like the *Ode to the West Wind,* in which he said: "O Oil, make me thy conduit, even as the earth is!" It would be a poem of the will, and Mr. Rich-

ards would have a perfect right to test the scientific efficiency of the formula urged by the poem.

It is not with this kind of poetry, but with another
kind that is not a poetry of the will, that I am concerned;
and I have been offering a few commonplaces about its
neglect by our advanced critics. Genuine poetry has been
written in most ages—including the present—but it is a
sort of poetry that was written most completely by
Shakespeare. It is the sort of poetry that our "capitalist"
and "communist" allegorists have forgotten how to read.
When a Humanist remarks that Shakespeare merely presented life without interpreting it; when a communist
says that Shakespeare was a "capitalist" poet because, in
his plays, the lower classes are shown as buffoons, we
must remember that in each case we are being told precisely the same thing: that poetry is a document to be
used by the social will.

I have sketched some aspects of the poetry of the will,
which in the last century and a half has taken two direc-
tions that I will summarize again. First, the optimism of
science, either pure or social science, an uncritical and
positive Platonism. Secondly, the negative Platonism of
the romantic spirit, a pessimistic revolt of the individual
against the optimism of the scientific will. The quality of
volition is practical in each case. But for isolated figures
like Landor and Dickinson in the last century, and a few
today, the creative spirit has been shunted off into ob-
scurity by the heresy of the will.

The quality of poetic vision that I have already in this

essay named, with respect to the two forms of will, the middle ground of vision, and, with respect to itself, the vision of the whole, is not susceptible of logical demonstration. We may prepare our minds for its reception by the logical elimination of error. But the kind of criticism that dominates our intellectual life is that of the French mathematician who, after reading a tragedy by Racine, asked: *"Qu'est ce que cela prouve?"* It proves nothing; it creates the totality of experience in its quality; and it has no useful relation to the ordinary forms of action.

Since I have not set out to prove an argument, but to look into arguments that seem to me to be wrong, I will state a conclusion as briefly as possible: that poetry finds its true usefulness in its perfect inutility, a focus of repose for the will-driven intellect that constantly shakes the equilibrium of persons and societies with its unrelieved imposition of partial formulas upon the world. When the will and its formulas are put back into an implicit relation with the whole of our experience, we get the true knowledge which is poetry. It is the "kind of knowledge which is really essential to the world, the true content of its phenomena, that which is subject to no change, and therefore is known with equal truth for all time." Let us not argue about it. It is here for those who have eyes to see.

HUMANISM AND NATURALISM

I F the necessity for virtue could tell us how to practise it, we should be virtuous overnight. For the case of the American Humanists against modern culture is damaging to the last degree. The truth of their indictment, negatively considered, cannot be denied. But this is not enough.

There is a widespread belief that the doctrines of Humanism are fundamentally sound. It would be truer to say that they are only partly and superficially so, and that they are being rejected for superficial reasons—the Humanists are dogmatic, they ignore contemporary literature, they lack the "æsthetic sense." These limitations go deeper. Humanism is obscure in its sources; it is even more ambiguous as to the kind of authority to which it appeals. And yet believers in tradition, reason, and authority will approach the writings of Messrs. Babbitt,* More and Foerster with more than an open mind; they will have in advance the conviction that

the rightful concern of man is his humanity, his world of value . . . that marks him off from a merely quantitative order;

but, after a great deal of patient reading, they will come

* In preparing this essay for the press I have not considered it appropriate to notice the death of Irving Babbitt by changing my references to him to the past tense. I reprint the essay because the best of Babbitt is still alive.

away with that conviction—and with no more than that conviction. They will have got no specific ideas about values—that is to say, they will have gained no medium for acquiring them; and such a medium, they will hold, is morally identical with the values themselves. Values are not suspended in the air to be plucked. They will reflect, suspiciously, that the vague method of the Humanist resembles the vague method of the so-called Romantic in the very respect in which agreement or difference is fundamental: the Humanist pursues Humanism for its own sake—or, say, restraint for restraint's sake, or proportion for proportion's sake—and while this is doubtless better than pursuing disorder for disorder's sake, the authority of the worthier pursuit is no clearer than that of the baser. His doctrine of restraint does not look to *unity,* but to abstract and external *control*—not to a solution of the moral problem, but to an attempt to get the moral results of unity by main force, by a kind of moral Fascism.

The reader will decide, moreover, that this defect of the Humanist is a central one and that, critically examined, it will turn out to be the philosophical plight of the so-called naturalist. Doctrinal differences in themselves may be negligible; the man who supposes himself a naturalist may practice the Humanistic virtues (Montaigne): the Humanist in doctrine may exhibit the method of naturalism (More). But if the appearance of mere doctrine is deceptive, the use of a method cannot be. The Humanists have no method. How, under the special complexities and distractions of the modern world, they intend to make good their values they do not say; they simply urge them. And this discrepancy between doctrine and method their hardier readers will find adequately described in Book II, Chapter IV, of the *Nicomachean Ethics:*

. . . yet people in general do not perform these actions, but taking refuge in talk they flatter themselves they are philosophizing, and that they will so be good men: acting in truth very like those sick people who listen to the doctor with great attention but do nothing that he tells them: just as these people cannot be well bodily under such a course of treatment, neither can those be mentally by such philosophizing.

The Humanists have listened not only to one doctor but to a great many doctors, and they tell us what they say; but they have not learned, and they cannot teach us, how to take the medicine.

I propose, in the first place, therefore, to analyze the position held by those Humanists in whom the minimum of doctrine appears: I mean by the minimum of doctrine that their thought refuses to exceed the moralistic plane: they steadily repudiate all religious and philosophical support. The Humanists of this type are Babbitt and Foerster. Secondly, I shall try to discover how this Humanism differs, if it differ, from that of Mr. More, who appears to lean heavily upon religious values. If Humanism shall save itself—that is to say, if it shall find a method—what is the position into which it will be logically driven?

I

The Humanism formulated by Mr. Norman Foerster in the last chapter of his *American Criticism* is actually a summary of the views of Professor Babbitt. The summary is, of course, an over-simplification, and does scant justice to Professor Babbitt's intellectual resourcefulness; yet I think it contains the fundamental scheme of his position. (It omits one of his chief difficulties, which I will bring out in a moment.) The assumptions of Humanism, according to Mr. Foerster, are as follows:

(1) ". . . that assumptions are necessary." Foerster points out the self-deception of the naturalist, or the anti-authoritarian, who thinks he has got rid of assumptions.

(2) ". . . that the essential elements of human experience are precisely those which appear to conflict with the reality explored by naturism. It [Humanism] recognizes, indeed, the service of naturism . . . in showing the power of the natural man's impulses."

(3) ". . . the central assumption of humanism is that of a dualism of man and nature . . . the rightful concern of man is his humanity, his world of value and quality that marks him off from a merely quantitative natural order."

(4) "Finally, humanism assumes the freedom of the will to conform to a standard of values, as opposed to the deterministic assumption of naturism."

From these assumptions Mr. Foerster proceeds to a doctrine which I reproduce in a greatly abridged form:

(1) An adequate human standard calls for *completeness*. This includes "natural" human nature.

(2) But is also calls for *proportion:* it demands the harmony of the *parts with the whole.*

(3) The complete, proportionate standard may be said to consist of the *normally* or *typically human.*

(4) Although such an ethos has never existed, it has been approximated in the great ages of the past. Foerster looks mainly to Greece, but he includes the Romans, Vergil, and Horace; the Christians, Jesus, Paul, Augustine, others; the Orientals, Buddha and Confucius; the moderns, Shakespeare, Milton, Goethe. (But he has misgivings about Shakespeare.)

(5) Unlike Romanticism, Humanism is true to its Hellenic origin in its faith in *reason.* It seeks to deal positively with the whole of human experience, including those elements of experience that do *not* fall within the scope of what it termed science.

(6) Unlike the conceptions of life that grow out of science, Humanism seeks to press beyond reason by the use of *intuition* or *imagination* . . . the human or ethical imagination, as distinguished from the natural or pathetic imagination, which is below the reason.

(7) The ultimate ethical principle is that of restraint or control.

(8) This center to which Humanism refers everything . . . is the reality that gives rise to religion. But pure Humanism is content to describe it *in physical terms* . . . it hesitates to pass beyond its experimental knowledge to the dogmatic affirmations of any of the great religions . . . it holds that *supernatural revelation must be tested by the intellect* . . . it should be clear that Humanism, like Greek philosophy, *begins with science* and *not* with religion.

Now Mr. Foerster says that human values are those which *appear* to conflict (do they or do they not?) with the reality explored by naturism; and yet Humanism demands the cultivation of all human nature, including "natural" human nature. He says, too, that Humanism rejects the elements of experience that fall within the "scope of what is termed science." However this may be, Humanism puts its faith in reason (because of its Hellenic origin) and it is based upon science, and yet it is unlike the conceptions of life that grow out of science. It demands a dualism of man and nature opposed to the monistic assumption of naturism. But how, it may be asked, is this dualism to be preserved along with that other requirement of a "harmony of the parts with the *whole*"? Mr. Foerster has just denounced the monistic whole. And, further, it may be asked, upon which side of the duality does reason take its stand? If science is naturism, and reason science, the question answers itself.

Humanism is based upon science, which is naturism, and yet it is unlike the conceptions of life that grow out of science. Here it may be asked upon which science Mr. Foerster performs his miracle of accepting rejection? Is it just *science*? Or is it an unconscious attitude whose vision of reality is mechanism, a popular version of genuine science? In this case, it is the quantitative natural order of which he speaks. But how did it get quantified? Is it *naturally* quantified? The only plausible answer is that it was quantified by Mr. Foerster's kind of reason, but that being unaware of this he can, with an effective "chaser" handy, drink "reason" off neat.

The chaser is the "ethical imagination," which presses beyond reason. We have seen that he puts his faith in reason, and it is difficult to see why he wishes a faith beyond faith, or why he selects this particular super-faith: he refuses to press beyond reason in favor of religion.

His desire to go beyond reason is his desire to escape from naturalism. This conception of reason is contradictory. The mere desire to get out of jail will not unlock the gate, and you remain a prisoner: Mr. Foerster remains a naturalist. He says that "supernatural intuition" —the phrase smacks of romantic Bergsonism—must be tested by the intellect. It is, thus, distinct from the intellect, not implicit in its action—a dichotomy that puts Mr. Foerster into the hands of the nineteenth-century Romantics whose evil he sets out to undo. This is the naturalistic, eighteenth-century "rationalistic" conception of imagination: irrational constructions of reality which "reason" (naturalism) may break down and reject. When Mr. Foerster says that religion and the imagination must be tested by the intellect, he therefore means tested by naturalism. For naturalism contains the only idea of reason that is available to the Humanist.

If this were not true, the Humanist would not be forced to exceed reason. Mr. Foerster is a century behind the thought of his age: he is a romantic post-Kantian who can find no way out of mechanism but imaginative illusion. This imaginative illusion was the ethical imagination which Schiller found to be the only way out of scientism, and its origin is betrayed by Schiller's description of it as the ideal representation of Causality. The difficulty for Mr. Foerster and Schiller is the question, How is this moral imagination to get itself moralized? You get nowhere by saying that the ethical imagination is above the reason, the pathetic imagination below; you have first to give them a motive for being what they are; without this you have a logical hypostasy, and the above and the below become "picture-thinking."

Mr. Foerster will have to decide to be scientifically reasonable, or not to be scientifically reasonable, whether he wants the parts to harmonize with the whole, or whether he rejects the whole for a dualism of the parts. He cannot have reason checking the natural and still keep it natural. Unless he can make up his mind, his dualism is merely verbal. He is expecting naturalism to unnaturalize itself —or, in other words, the imagination to make itself moral.

But perhaps after all he has a way out: there is one card remaining to be played, and it may turn out to be an ace. Now, the ultimate ethical principle is restraint or control, and the motivation of the ethical imagination is restraint; or at least it acts under the motive of restraint in order to achieve the "normally or typically human." This is the ideal towards which Humanism strives, deriving its principles from ancient approximations of the ideal. But, if the ethical imagination is the instrument for creating the typically human, what is its motive for doing so? Is it restraint? Or is it restraining morality? Or is it restrained restraint? I hope I do not press this too far. You have got to go back to certain prior conditions under which an ethical imagination is possible. If the ethical imagination *is* imagination it must deal with images; but the Humanists give us only a digest of the ancient cultures; they leave to abstract inference a conception of the particular culture in which the humane life may be lived. However wicked the personal life of Villon may have been, his imagination, under the conditions of his age, was bound to be ethical because it had a pervasive authority for being so; it could not escape this authority in some form.

It has been pointed out that Mr. Foerster's quantified nature has been quantified by his own kind of reason, and that he is, in fact, a naturalist. This brings us to one of the chief difficulties of Professor Babbitt's position.

Now Professor Babbitt, in order to escape from a passive Rousseauism, constantly opposes to it, notably in *Rousseau and Romanticism,* the ideal of the man of action, *"who, as a result of his moral choices based on due deliberation, choices in which he is moved primarily by a regard for his own happiness, has quelled the unruly impulses of his lower nature."* Again, in *Democracy and Leadership,* he writes: *"To be completely moral one must be positive and critical."*

This positive intellect, split off from the harmony of action possible to the unified, but not to the deliberately controlled, mind, is the very intellect that has supported naturalism throughout its history. It has created the self-seeking industrialist who *is moved primarily by a regard for his own happiness.* Professor Babbitt, of course, sees that this man *goes too far;* yet *how* far is *too* far? He has only the positive and critical intellect to tell him, and the best this can do is to set up an arbitrary limit to its own self-seeking activity—another instance of naturalism trying to unnaturalize itself. The stopping-place is pointed out by a study of the "wisdom of the ages," but it should be remembered that this wisdom must be discovered by the positive and critical intellect, which is supposed to use it against itself.

This, I believe, exposes the negative basis of Professor Babbitt's morality. The good man is he who "refrains from doing" what the "lower nature dictates," and he need do nothing positive. He merely refrains from complete action on the naturalistic level while remaining on that level.

It is clear that this is the source of Mr. Foerster's dilemma—whether to suffer the slings and arrows of outrageous naturalism by "cultivating" it or to reject it altogether. Neither Professor Babbitt nor Mr. Foerster conceives a unified "ethical imagination" moving harmoniously from the center outwards. They hypostatize it as a mediator, like Malebranche's deity, an occasional visitor to the mind to be called in or not, at will. The mind is a mechanical parallelism of moral and natural forces arbitrarily distinct. The ethical force, being the mere negation of the natural, does not positively oppose the supposed enemy because he is really his friend. For this parallelism comes down to an attempt on the part of the natural force to control itself by a law of its own making—a law as various as the individualists who try to formulate it.

Now the moralist in this predicament is not the Aristotelian moralist—and I seem to remember that Professor Babbitt aligns himself with the Stagirite. Professor Babbitt's moral man deliberately undertakes to do, say, four good deeds a day to *offset* his evil impulses, which thus are counterbalanced but not transformed—just as the late Henry Clay Frick collected pictures to offset his transactions in steel. But the Aristotelian deliberately undertakes the doing of "goods" not at all, for to him there are no goods distinct from the performance of his ordinary obligations, such as being polite to his enemies or digging ditches, which become moral goods only in so far as the man is a unified moral agent. His morality is not explicit but implicit in his specific moral acts, which are moral or immoral according to his implicit moral quality. Professor Babbitt's explicit morality is the finger of the Dutch boy in the dyke, or the man sitting gingerly on the keg of dynamite lest it explode. The modern problem is desperate, and Professor Babbitt recommends the police force.

From this position comes Babbitt's illuminating hierarchy of social values. Men should be materially rewarded for three kinds of labor, and in this order: (1) moral work, (2) intellectual work, and (3) manual work. The intellectual and the laborer are not doing moral work because they do not, while attending to their specific jobs, strive to propagate an explicit morality! Thus moral work is not qualitative but quantitative, and can be measured; it should be measurably rewarded. Doubtless it should; but meanwhile the honest laborer may be doing as much moral work as the professional moralist, and with considerably less self-righteous snobbery. Professor Babbitt's unshakable belief in the "war in the cave," interpreted through a categorical rather than a functional psychology, dooms us forever to a kind of Manichean ill-breeding.

The conditions that should underlie the ethical imagination are by no means fulfilled by Mr. Foerster's doctrinaire summary of Sophocles, or of Vergil, or of Augustine, or his summary of these summaries, taken alone. You cannot get out of them a philosophy or a religion; for literature is no substitute for philosophy and religion. It is this vague understanding on the part of the Humanists of the nature of philosophy, it is their lack of an exact logical and philosophical discipline, which betrays them, not only into the muddy reasoning that we have just seen; it leads them to expect to find in literature, ancient or modern, an explicit philosophy sufficient unto itself— a philosophy, in short, that does not already exist in some purer instead of a derived and literary form. They ask us, in effect, to burn the *Summa,* and to study Aquinas, as *Aquinas,* in Dante.

The belief held at various times since the Renaissance that the ancients are models of attitude and value is innocent enough; and it was useful so long as the classics could be assimilated to a living center of judgment and feeling. But, without this center, you get eclecticism— you get Professor Babbitt. And the sole defense of eclecticism is naturalistic—that is to say, it assumes the capacity of the mind to combine mechanically upon a *tabula rasa* a variety of unlike elements into a unity. We know that mechanical interaction, were it possible, could not yield

a whole, but an aggregate. It expects Sophocles to fuse
with Vergil without an agency of fusion. The Humanist
conception of literature is mechanical and naturalistic.

This is because its ingrained habit of mind is mechanical. The habit is the decisively important thing. The way
one uses a method is, in the end, the doctrine, and not
the literal significance of the doctrine's terms. The Humanistic method, its ingrained habit of mind, is fundamentally opposed to its doctrine, and the sole condition
under which this doctrine could be made good would
be a center of life philosophically and morally consistent
with it. Until this center is found, and not pieced together
eclectically at the surface, Humanism is an attempt to do
mechanically—that is, naturalistically—what should be
done morally.

Its idea of the "past"—of tradition—is infinite regression. When it is asked for "authority," it is constantly
driven back from one position to another. We arrive at
last at the "wisdom of the ages"—but can this wisdom be
taken in and evaluated by a mind that has no way of
knowing that it is wise? Professor Babbitt is a learned
and distinguished man, and he may be wise. But for this
we have only his word, since his morality, as we have
seen, is only an arbitrarily individualistic *check upon itself:* his wisdom is a naturalistically historical recovery of
the past.

The idea of infinite regression to authoritative judgment inheres in the thought of Foerster and Babbitt, and
it is probably the subtlest fallacy to which Humanism is

committed. It takes all the *time* out of the past and all
the concreteness out of the present. This fallacy is due
to an unconscious transformation of the idea of an increasingly distant temporal past into the idea of a logical
series which is quite timeless. This is another pitfall of
picture-thinking: time is confused with logical succession,
which, of course, may run in any "direction" or all direc-
tions at once. The Humanist thus convinces himself that
his logical series is a temporal past, and as such affords
him a stopping-place—some fixed doctrine or some self-
contained wisdom of the ages. But there can be no absolute in a logical series because all its terms are equal
and it never ends.

Now the logical series is quantitative, the abstraction of
space. The temporal series is, on the other hand, space
concrete. Concrete, temporal experience implies the existence of a temporal past, and it is the foundation of the
religious imagination; that is to say, the only way to think
of the past independently of Mr. Foerster's naturalism is
to think religiously; and conversely, the only way to
think religiously is to think in time. Naturalistic science
is timeless. A doctrine based upon it, whether explicitly
or not, can have no past, no idea of tradition, no fixed
center of life. The "typically human" is a term that cannot exist apart from some other term; it is not an absolute; it is fluid and unfixed.

To de-temporize the past is to reduce it to an abstract
lump. To take from the present its concrete fullness is to
refuse to let standards work from the inside. It follows

that "decorum" must be "imposed" from above. Thus there are never specific moral problems (the subject matter of the arts) but only fixed general doctrines without subject matter—that is to say, without "nature."

The "historical method," says Mr. Foerster, rose in the age of naturalism, but he wishes to keep it as a valuable adjunct to Humanism. It is a wish that Humanism may rise upon its own débris, the miracle of naturalism unnaturalizing itself. Men cannot be naturalists with one half of the mind, Humanists with the other; or does Mr. Foerster desire the growth of two co-operating classes— naturalists and Humanists? The convictions of the one class are bound to undermine those of the other. The "historical method" has always been the anti-historical method. Its aim is to contemporize the past. Its real effect is to de-temporize it. The past becomes a causal series, and timeless; and as a quantitative abstraction (as Foerster himself sees) valueless. Are we to infer that, after the historical naturalists have done their work, the Humanist will intercede and evaluate? This is the Victorian and naturalistic illusion all over again—that good may somehow be the "goal of ill."

Professor Babbitt has acutely charged the experimental moderns with not being experimental enough—they have not, he says, questioned the assumptions of their time, but swallowed them whole. He himself continues to experiment, but, as Mr. Eliot has pointed out, we cannot go on experimenting indefinitely. The reason why Professor Babbitt remains an inveterate experimenter is that he, in his turn, has not been philosophical enough. He constantly repudiates "æsthetics," which he believes to be a trivial decoration of moral doctrine; yet in literature the æsthetic approach is necessarily the philosophical approach. The dilemma between decoration externally imposed and imposed morality is false, and Professor Babbitt merely prefers the pot to the kettle.

The Socratic method, which he and Mr. Foerster after him apply so ably to contemporary society, is a method only, and it may be used by the Humanist and his critic alike. Torn out of the Platonic Dialogues, it is an instrument for the exposure of contradiction; it brings with it no motive for the exposure; it yields no absolutes. This will be made clearer in a brief analysis of the Humanism of Paul Elmer More.

II

If Professor Babbitt's Humanism is eclectic, Mr. More's is equally so—but the apparent synthesis takes place on the religious plane. Humanists like Babbitt and Foerster have to meet the problem of access to truth beyond the personality: it is obvious that Babbitt is a sound man, that his views are sound because he is; but there is no other guarantee of the soundness of his views. He is a "personality," and there is nothing to do about personality but to feel that it is sound or unsound. Mr. More, however, compels us to answer the question: Is his religion as a source of moral authority sound or unsound?

The problem is harder than that of personality, but in

the end it is the same. What, in the first place, is Mr. More's religion?* Is it Christianity? It is possible that it is. He has written time and again about the insight afforded us by Christian writers, and to them he has brought no inconsiderable insight of his own. There is also, according to Mr. More, a profound insight in Plato —perhaps the profoundest. Again, his studies in the Hindu religions and philosophies have stimulated him to some of his best and most sympathetic writing: the Hindus teach a deep religious dualism. Mr. More's *Studies of Religious Dualism* is a kind of breviary of the good he finds in half a dozen or more religious attitudes. The question remains: which of these religions is Mr. More's? The answer to this, I believe, is: Mr. More's religion is Mr. More's.

Now one of Mr. More's critics has justly called the five volumes of *The Greek Tradition* an "original and profound work"; yet does its originality and profundity bear upon the question of religious authority—the sole question that I am putting to Mr. More's religious writings? However, Mr. More's defender indirectly attempts to answer this very question; he says: *"The Christ of the New Testament* [contains] an exact and unmistakable explanation of his [More's] acceptance of the historic Christian revelation." I have examined this explanation as well as Mr. More's other religious writings; yet what "acceptance" means is not clear, for his Christianity excludes be-

---

* I should like to remind the reader that this discussion of Mr. More was written in 1929.

lief in the Miracles and the Virgin Birth. There is a detailed analysis yet to be made of his religious books; still I think that my conclusion will be found to be correct: the historic revelation that Mr. More has accepted is largely one of his own contrivance. It is revelation on his own terms—revelation as revealed by Mr. More. It is a reconstruction of the historical elements in a pattern satisfactory to the needs of "independent faith" (his phrase), the authority for which is to be found solely in his own books.

He has written a good deal on religion, but it is not easy to put one's finger on his conception of it. Because of the discrepancy between the individualism of his religion and the dogmatism of his judgments his explicit statements on the subject tend to be vague. And yet he does have definite ideas. Their most significant expression is in incidental commentary. About twenty years ago he took to task an interpreter of the Forest Philosophers for trying

to convert into hard intellectualism what was at bottom a religious and thoroughly human experience.

Is intellectualism incompatible with religion? If the experience was thoroughly human, was it also religious? Mr. More thinks that it was. If intellectualism has no place in religion, where does it belong? Mr. More's reply to this is undoubtedly Mr. Foerster's conception of reason: reason is the exclusive privilege of what the Humanists call naturism. Religion is an indefinite, unutterable belief. Mr. More, as well as Babbitt and Foerster, cannot get out of this notion of reason. Now, if religion is not allowed to reason, what may it do? Shall it be contented with visions? I think that Mr. More would say no; but he could not rationally say it. Mr. More repeats implicitly the dilemma of Babbitt and Foerster—and a dilemma is very different from a dualism. You have on the one hand scientific naturalism; on the other, irrational belief —the "illusion of a higher reality" that is only an illusion. It is the familiar doctrine of the *philosophe,* that the religious or ethical imagination is an aberration of the intellect, of naturalism. Mr. More would say that the religious and the human join in opposing the natural. But if the religious and the human combine in the present state of Mr. More's religion, which is individualistic, he is opposing naturalism with opposition. You cannot overcome naturalism with "illusion" or an individualistic faith; the illusion and the individualism are properties of the thing to be overcome. In spite of Mr. More's religious attitude, most of my criticism of Babbitt and Foerster applies to him.

Mr. More's dilemma is implicit throughout *Christ the Word,* and it becomes explicit in an essay entitled *An Absolute and an Authoritative Church (The Criterion,* July 1929). Harassed by the demon of the absolute, he tries to find religious authority apart from the Protestant claim of infallibility for the biblical texts, on the one hand, and, on the other, from the Roman claim of absolute interpretation of these texts. The solution of the problem seems to lie in the Eastern and the Anglican Churches, which offer "the kind of revelation which neither in book nor in Church is absolute, but in both book and Church possesses a sufficient authority." The merit of any particular church is beside my point, but Mr. More's idea of authority is very much to it, and he fails to make it clear. He admits that his authority may bring "the reproach of uncertainty," and the reader must conclude that the uncertainty is rooted in his persistently independent faith. The essay is a summary of Mr. More's religious thought, and it is forthright and fearless; but it ends in vague appreciation of tradition tempered by individualism. The dilemma of absolutes remains untouched because Mr. More seems to lack the philosophical impulse to think himself out of it.

He gives us, in the first chapter of *Studies of Religious Dualism,* something of his religious history up to that time (1909). He had repudiated Calvinism. He was drifting, but suddenly he found a book that initiated him into the "mysteries of independent faith"—the kind of faith, one observes, that the romantic, the naturist, the Rousseauist, has supported all along. Now just how much independence was necessary? Mr. More had to make his decision individualistically, and he had, like Professor Babbitt, no way of knowing when he came to more than a personal stop.

His critics have accused him of a defective "æsthetic sense"; he has seemed to be preoccupied with the content of literature; he has little to say of style, almost nothing, except what he says impatiently, of the craft of writing from the point of view of the writer. With Professor Babbitt, he never permits us to forget his conviction that the problems of craft are secondary and "æsthetic" and that, if the writer is virtuous, the writing will take care of itself. The reply to this is not that such confusion of thought is unworthy of Mr. More—which it is. It is not enough to oppose to it an equal confusion—that his is due to a lack of æsthetic perception. His failure to understand the significance of style is a failure to understand most of the literature that he has read. It is his intention to examine the "doctrine" of a given work in the light of his own. We have just seen that it is difficult to find out what Mr. More's doctrine is. With what is literature, then, to coincide? Mr. More entertains false hopes of literature; he expects it to be a philosophy and a religion because, in his state of "independent faith," he has neither a definite religion nor a definite philosophy prior to the book he happens to be reading.

In *The Demon of the Absolute* he remarks that he is not concerned at the moment with artistic means; only with "results." This distinction runs all through Mr. More's writings; he is not concerned with the letter of religion or of literature—the means through which it exists and is preserved, the religion or the literature itself. Religious results, separate from religious means, become—if they become anything—independent faith. Literary results, that is, the didactic paraphrase of a work of literature, challenge or support independent morality. In either case the full content of the literary or religious text is left behind. When Mr. More tells us that a writer has a sound moral attitude, he may be right, but there is no reason to believe that he may not be wrong. His judgments, for us, are thus neither right nor wrong: strictly speaking they are meaningless. He cannot cite his independent faith because he has no text outside himself; it is rationally inarticulate; there is no way to communicate it.

Nevertheless, Mr. More evidently supposes that he is conveying it; else he would not continue to write books. His reasons for this supposition not only command attention; they are of great interest in themselves. Mr. More is, among other things, a Platonist. What is a Platonist? Is he a man who believes what Plato believed? Or is he a man who uses the Socratic method for the exposure of contradiction? If he is the latter, to what end does he expose contradiction? Since Mr. More obviously believes things that Plato did not, he is, if he be a Platonist at all, one by virtue of his use of the Socratic method. But why does he use it? There is only one answer: for the support of independent faith.

And yet he constantly draws upon Plato for quotations and analogies (he has written a book on the subject); he has the air of delivering his opinions from quoted authority. But owing to the distracting influence of the other authorities—Christ, the Forest Philosophers—that compose his independent faith, it is difficult to ascertain just how authoritative, at a given moment, Plato is. The real authority at all times, of course, is Mr. More. I need hardly point out that Mr. More logically drives himself into the position of spiritual exile and, if he speak at all, of arrogance to which he has consigned the romantic enemy.

The belief in the authority of Plato when More is the actual authority explains the poor quality of his literary judgments. Moral judgments are never more irresponsible than when the judge supposes that the high and mighty of the past are behind him. Mr. More is a man whose critical habits are not subject to the purification and correction of specific objective standards, and the delusion that they are only increases their irresponsibility. In the name of restraint he is able to evoke the limit of his personal distastes.

Mr. More's fallacy is identical, as I have said, with that of the non-religious Humanists. Because he cannot find an adequate conception of concrete tradition (experience) in terms of authority (reason), he gives us abstract, timeless, rootless, habitual ideas that closely resemble, in structure, the rationalism of the naturists. Authority in More becomes the spectral sorites of infinite regress. There is no conception of religion as preserved, organized experience; you have a mechanism of moral ideas. Take this passage by Mr. More:

> True art is humanistic rather than naturalistic; and its gift of high and permanent pleasure is the response of our own breast to the artist's delicately revealed sense of that divine control moving like the spirit of God upon the face of the waters.
>
> So far I seem to see my way clear. If you should ask me by what rhetorical devices or by what instrument of representation one poem . . . appeals more successfully than another to the

higher faculty within us, how, for instance, Milton's *Paradise Lost* accomplishes this end better than Blackmore's *King Arthur,* though *both poems were written with equally good intentions* (italics mine); I would reply frankly that the solution of this problem of the imagination may be beyond my powers of critical analysis.

The first part of this passage is a fair example of the pulpit rhetoric into which Mr. More plunges when he speaks of the relation of literature to religion, and the reason why his thought is vague is that, like Professor Babbitt, he has not been philosophical enough; he has not examined his own assumptions. It is difficult to distinguish, in the above quotation, any reason why true art is Humanistic; for the "high and permanent pleasure" and "the divine control" are only pleasant ways of naming mechanical habits of thought. Mr. More has never philosophized his ideas into ultimates —those fixed yet interpretative, flexible positions from the viewpoint of which the ghost of naturalism and the otherwise disembodied spirit of morality become, not *things,* but experience in the life of man.

As Mr. Eliot has pointed out in the case of Babbitt, More ignores the conditions out of which a book emerges. These conditions alone realize the author's ideas; they alone contribute morality, not an abstract, but a specific morality in terms of experience, to the work of literature. More cannot tell us why Milton is superior to Blackmore because his sole idea of the mind is that of a mechanism of moral ideas. The intentions of the two poems being equally good, he cannot understand why their equal morality does not moralize the pieces into an equal excellence; because moral ideas are *things* they ought to be as efficient in one place as in another. Mr. More conceives literature, first, as a mechanism of ideas; then, as a mechanism of books themselves; literature is a timeless, self-perpetuating machine set in motion in an infinite past which, being timeless, is no past at all. To be another Dante you have only to believe that his ideas, his "results," are good, and to identify them in some undefined sense with your own moral habits.

Mr. More's doctrine is morality for morality's sake, and if art for art's sake has always been an outrage upon reason, his position is no less so. Rationally there is little to choose between them.

His view of style as rhetorical devices is, then, perfectly consistent: the devices have no necessary connection with what is being said; like morality, they are superimposed. Morality being automatically moral, moral values are moral before they are communicated; the style merely dresses them up. But how can there be abstract results apart from the means—apart from the medium which, under concrete conditions, fixes the values in experience? Style—the way values are apprehended—is the technique for validating them. Mr. More's theory logically ends in never uttering another word.

Because he cannot take the philosophical view he sees naturalism as the worship of instinct, license, self—all the things, in fact, that a respectable citizen of the United States for reasons of social habit would not permit himself to do. This is admirable enough—but it is not philosophical. No one in his senses would deny that François Villon was a person of instinct, that he was pitiably engrossed in his own self, that he was a licentious fellow; no one in his senses would call François Villon a naturalist. The point at issue lies where Humanism cannot take hold of it. The anti-naturalist is still a naturalist, if he cannot get off his naturalistic plane. Mr. More is a naturalist because he presents a mechanical view of experience. A doctrine is not a method, and until it can be made one, the Humanists are "flattering themselves they are philosophizing and that they will so be good men."

III

How shall we know when we have values?—a more difficult problem than the mere conviction that we need them. There is no such thing as pure value, nor are there values separate from the means of creating and preserving them. There are certain definite ways in which men have had access to value in the past (the Humanists tell us that Dante had values, but not how he got them); but our problem is, Have we any of those ways now? If we have, how may they be used? Is there a condition or are there several conditions that must be met before we may use them?

We have seen the assumptions of the Humanists. The assumptions of this essay are that Humanism is not enough, and that if the values for which the Humanist pleads are to be made rational, even intelligible, the background of an

objective religion, a universal scheme of reference, is necessary. There should be a living center of action and judgment, such as we find in the great religions, which in turn
grew out of this center. The act of "going into the Church"
is not likely to supply the convert with it. Yet, for philosophical consistency, this is what the Humanists should do.
It is clear that this essay urges the claim of no special religion, and it is in no sense a confession of faith; but the connection between the Reformation and the rise of Naturalism, and what I conceive the religious imagination to be,
point to the position that the Humanists must occupy if
they wish to escape intellectual suicide. The religious unity
of intellect and emotion, of reason and instinct, is the sole
technique for the realization of values.

The virtue of religion is its successful representation of
the problem of evil. The Humanists recognize immoral
conduct but they ignore evil in the religious sense. We
have seen how Mr. Foerster, wishing at once to cultivate
natural human nature and to reject it, could not decide
how far he wished to go in either direction. This was because his dualism was verbal; there were no really opposed principles; there was simply an infinite number
of points on the same scale. And thus his opposition between Quality and Quantity was verbal too; it was Quantity versus Quantity, presided over by rootless Restraint,
the referee who checked nothing but coherent thought.
The Humanists tell us that somehow we have to do with
Quality, yet since for them nature is the qualified nature of scientism and the mind is a quantified machine

of moral ideas, it is difficult to see where Quality comes from. The Humanists seem to use the word to mean something "better" than something else—the philosophical level at which the fashionable tailor uses it.

There is, then, a preliminary question to be asked: What is the source of qualitative experience? Both horns of his dualism being reduced to Quantity, the Humanist cannot tell us; and that is why much of his criticism gives us the feeling that he expects us to pluck values out of the air. Since the Humanist has not been philosophically hardy enough to work out of the naturalistic version of nature, which he naïvely accepts; since, in fact, he cannot root the concept of nature as Quantity out of his mind, his idea of Quality is irresponsible, foot-loose, highly transcendental in a kind of Concord sense.

The source of Quality is nature itself because it is the source of experience. It is only by holding to an idea that leaves nature an open realm of Quality that experience is made possible at all; and, conversely, experience alone is the road to Quality. If a zoölogist sees a certain Philippine cobra he doubtless says, *"Naja samaransis."* The snake is merely an instance of the quantification of nature. The head-hunter, however, has a more vivid feeling for the unique possibilities of the particular cobra; it may bite him; it may give him the evil eye—both richly qualitative experiences. For the Humanist, *opposing* Quality to nature, has got it on the wrong side of his duality. Pure Quality would be pure evil, and it is only through the means of our recovery from a lasting immersion in it, it is only by maintaining the precarious balance upon the point of collapse into Quality, that any man survives his present hour: pure quality is pure disintegration. The scientist says, *"Naja samaransis";* Mr. More, a cadence of the same theme—"Immoral"; Quality is quantified before we ever see it as Quality; and nature becomes a closed system of abstraction in which man is deprived of all experience whatever and, by being so deprived, reduced to an abstraction himself.

The religious attitude is the very sense (as the religious dogma is the definition) of the precarious balance of man upon the brink of pure Quality. But if you never have Quality, never have the challenge of evil, you have no religion—which is to say, you have no experience either. It is experience, immediate and traditional, fused—Quality and Quantity—which is the means of validating values.

Experience gives the focus to style, and style is the way anything is done. Rhetorical device is our abstract term for properties of style after style is achieved; they have never of themselves made one poem better than another.

Religion's respect for the power of nature lies in her contempt for knowledge of it; to quantify nature is ultimately to quantify ourselves. Religion is satisfied with the dogma that nature is evil, and that our recovery from it is mysterious ("grace"). For the abstraction of nature ends, as we have seen, with the destruction of the reality of time, and immediate experience being impossible, so do all ideas of tradition and inherited order become timeless and incoherent. It is the indispensable office of the religious imagination that it checks the abstracting tendency of the intellect in the presence of nature. Nature abstract becomes man abstract, and he is at last condemned to a permanent immersion in pure and evil Quality; he is forever condemned to it because he can no longer see it for what it is. He has no technique for dealing with evil. The protection of religion is the abstraction, not of nature, which so conceived would be the abstraction of abstraction, but of experience. It proposes a system of Quantity *against* nature; it is a quantitative version of the encounter between the head-hunter and the cobra. The organized meaning of the encounters of man and nature, which are temporal and concrete, is religious tradition, and though religious tradition is not exclusively the Church, it necessarily implies a way of life historically protected by the Church. The dogma acts for the recoil of the native from the snake: it is his technique for finding out the value of the encounter. Every such encounter is rich and unique in Quality: it is the temporal, never-recurring focus, the new triumph, the re-affirmation of the preserved experience of man. The modern Humanist, because of habitual reactions, recoils, but he has no reason for doing so, and his recoil is without value. He and the cobra are one: Quantity versus Quantity; nature against nature; snake against snake; or, for that matter, man against man.

It is the failure of the Humanist to get out of this dilemma which makes his literary criticism feeble and incomplete. Mr. Foerster says: "It is best to face the issue in all candor"—the issue being Shakespeare. This poet merely "presents" life; he does not "interpret" it. If I had never read Shakespeare and had not read the rest of Mr. Foerster's book, his distinction would sound plausible; but having read his book, I know what he means, which is something very different from what he thinks he means. He means that the mind of Shakespeare was not a mechanism of moral ideas. The Humanists quarrel with literature because it cannot give them a philosophy and a church; but they keep turning to literature because they cannot find these things elsewhere. You cannot have the sense of literature without the prior, specific, and self-sufficient sense of something else. Without this you expect too much of literature; you expect of it a religion and a philosophy; and by expecting of it the wrong thing, you violate it, and in the end you get from it less than it is meant to yield; you get neither literature nor religion, nor anything that is intelligible. You destroy literature without constructing a religion.

For, as M. Ramon Fernandez has recently said, Humanism should not pretend to be a "body of Doctrine"; it is "a resultant situation."

The American Humanists have tried to make the resultant situation its own background. Humanism is too ambitious, with insufficient preparation. (I do not mean erudition.) It tries to take a short cut to the resultant situation, and ignores the moral difficulty of imagining what the background should be; it is an effort to imitate by rote the natural product of culture; it is a mechanical formula for the recovery of civilization. It is the cart before the horse, and because it gets the "philosophy" in the wrong place, it invites philosophical attack. Humanism should be culture, but it may be a little untamed in the Humanists until, as the digging of graves for the grave diggers, custom hath made it in them a property of easiness.

THE PROFESSION OF LETTERS IN THE SOUTH

THE profession of letters in France dates, I believe, from the famous manifesto of Du Bellay and the Pléiade in 1549. It is a French habit to assume that France has supported a profession of letters ever since. There is no other country where the author is so much honored as in France, no other people in western culture who understand so well as the French the value of literature to the state. The national respect for letters begins far down in society. In a small town where I was unknown I was able to use a letter-of-credit without identification upon my word that I was a man of letters. The French have no illusions; we are not asked to believe that all French writers are respectable. The generation of Rimbaud and Verlaine was notoriously dissolute. French letters are a profession, as law, medicine, and the army are professions. Good writers starve and lead sordid lives in France as elsewhere; yet the audience for high literature is larger in France than in any other country; and a sufficient number of the best writers find a public large enough to sustain them as a class.

It goes somewhat differently with us. The American public sees the writer as a business man because it cannot see any other kind of man, and respects him according to his income. And, alas, writers themselves respect chiefly and fear only their competitors' sales. A big sale is a "success." How could it be otherwise? Our books are sold on a competitive market; it is a book market, but it is a luxury market; and luxury markets must be fiercely competitive. It is not that the natural depravity of the writer as fallen man betrays him into imitating the tone and standards of his market; actually he cannot find a public at all, even for the most lost of lost causes, the *succès d'estime,* unless he is willing to enter the competitive racket of publishing. This racket, our society being what it is, is a purely economic process, and literary opinion is necessarily manufactured for its needs. Its prime need is shoddy goods, because it must have a big, quick turnover. The overhead in the system is so high that the author gets only 10 to 15 per cent. of the gross. It is the smallest return that any producer gets in our whole economic system. To live even frugally, a novelist, if he does not do odd jobs on the side, must have a sale of about 30,000 copies every two years. Not only the publisher's but his turnover, too, must be quick. He has his own self-sweat shop. One must agree with Mr. Herbert Read, in the February, 1935, London *Mercury,* that authors under modern capitalism are a sweated class.

We have heard for years, we began hearing it as early as Jeffrey's review of the first *Hyperion,* that science is driving poetry to cover. I suppose it is; and we have the weight of Mr. I. A. Richards' arguments to prove it, and Mr. Max Eastman's weight, which is fairly light. Nineteenth-century science produced a race of "problem" critics and novelists. The new "social" point of view has multiplied the race. Literature needs no depth of background or experience to deal with problems; it needs chiefly the statistical survey and the conviction that society lives by formula, if not by bread alone. The nineteenth century began this *genre,* which has become the standard mode. I confess that I cannot decide whether "science" or the mass production of books, or the Spirit that made them both, has given us shoddy in literature. We were given, for example, Bennett and Wells; Millay and Masefield. And I surmise that not pure science but shoddy has driven the poets into exile, where, according to Eastman, they are "talking to themselves."

I shall not multiply instances. The trouble ultimately goes back to the beginnings of finance-capitalism and its creature, machine-production. Under feudalism the artist was a member of an organic society. The writer's loss of professional standing, however, set in before the machine, by which I mean the machine-age as we know it, appeared. It began with the rise of mercantile aristocracy in the eighteenth century. The total loss of professionalism in letters may be seen in our age—an age that remembers the extinction of aristocracy and witnesses the triumph of a more inimical plutocratic society.

If my history is not wholly incorrect, it must follow that our unlimited pioneering, the pretext of the newness of the country, and our low standards of education, do not explain the decline of the professional author. Pioneering became our way of industrial expansion, a method of production not special to us; we are a new country in so far as our industrialism gave to the latent vices of the

European mind a new opportunity; and our standards of education get lower with the increasing amount of money spent upon them. For my purposes, then, it is sufficient that we should look at the history of professionalism in letters in terms of the kinds of rule that European society, which includes American society, has had.

The South once had aristocratic rule; the planter class was about one fifth of the population; but the majority followed its lead. And so, by glancing at the South, we shall see in American history an important phase of the decline of the literary profession. There was, perhaps, in and around Boston, for a brief period, a group of professional writers. But not all of them, not even most of them, made their livings by writing. Even if they had, we should still have to explain why they were second-rate, and why the greatest of the Easterners, Hawthorne, Melville, Dickinson, had nothing to do with them or with the rising plutocracy of the East. But it is a sadder story still in the South. We had no Hawthorne, no Melville, no Emily Dickinson. We had William Gilmore Simms. We made it impossible for Poe to live south of the Potomac. Aristocracy drove him out. Plutocracy, in the East, starved him to death. I prefer the procedure of the South; it knew its own mind, knew what kind of society it wanted. The East, bent upon making money, could tolerate, as it still tolerates, any kind of disorder on the fringe of society as long as the disorder does not interfere with money-making. It did not know its own social mind; it was, and still is, plutocracy.

But let us look a little at the backgrounds of Southern literature. I say backgrounds, for the South is an immensely complicated region. It begins in the Northeast with southern Maryland; it ends with eastern Texas; it includes to the north even a little of Missouri. But that the people in this vast expanse of country have enough in common to bind them in a single culture cannot be denied. They often deny it themselves—writers who want to have something to jabber about, or other writers who want to offset the commercial handicap of being Southern; or newly rich persons in cities that would rather be like Pittsburgh than like New Orleans. It must be confessed that the Southern tradition has left no cultural landmark so conspicuous that the people may be reminded by it constantly of what they are. We lack a tradition in the arts; more to the point, we lack a literary tradition. We lack even a literature. We have just enough literary remains from the old régime to prove to us that, had a great literature risen, it would have been unique in modern times.

The South was settled by the same European strains as originally settled the North. Yet, in spite of war, reconstruction, and industrialism, the South to this day finds its most perfect contrast in the North. In religious and social feeling I should stake everything on the greater resemblance to France. The South clings (blindly) to forms (?) of European feeling and conduct that were crushed by the French Revolution and that, in England at any rate, are barely memories. How many Englishmen have told us that we still have the eighteenth-century amiability and consideration of manners, supplanted in their country by middle-class reticence and suspicion? And where, outside the South, is there a society that believes even covertly in the Code of Honor? This is not idle talk; we are assured of it by Professor H. C. Brearley, who, I believe, is one of the most detached students of Southern life. Where else in the modern world is the patriarchal family still innocent of the rise and power of other forms of society? Possibly in France; probably in the peasant countries of the Balkans and of Central Europe. Yet the "orientation"—let us concede the word to the University of North Carolina—the rise of new Southern points of view, even now in the towns, is tied still to the image of the family on the land. Where else does so much of the reality of the ancient land-society endure, along with the infatuated avowal of beliefs that are hostile to it? Where in the world today is there a more supine enthusiasm for being amiable to forces undermining the life that supports the amiability? The anomalous structure of the South, is, I think, finally witnessed by its religion. Doctor Poteat of South Carolina deplores a fact which he does not question, that only in the South does one find a convinced supernaturalism: it is nearer to Aquinas than to Calvin, Wesley, or Knox. Nor do we doubt that the conflict between modernism and fundamentalism is chiefly the impact of the new middle-class civilization upon the rural society; nor, moreover, should we allow ourselves to forget that philosophers of the State, from Sir Thomas

More to John C. Calhoun, were political defenders of the older religious community.

The key to unlock the Southern mind is, fortunately, like Bluebeard's, bloody and perilous; there is not the easy sesamé to the cavern of gaping success. The South has had reverses that permit her people to imagine what they might have been. (And only thus can people discover what they *are*.) Given the one great fact of the expanding plantation system at the dawn of the last century, which voice should the South have listened to? Jefferson, or Marshall, or Calhoun? I mean, which voice had the deepest moral and spiritual implications for the permanence of Southern civilization?

There was not time to listen to any voice very long. The great Southern ideas were strangled in the cradle, either by the South herself (for example, by too much quick cotton money in the Southwest) or by the Union armies. It is plain to modern historians of culture that peoples do not make, much less buy, a culture overnight; it takes time. Which view would have given the South a unified sense of its own destiny? Our modern "standard of living" is not a point of view, and it is necessary that a people should gather its experience round some seasoned point of view before it may boast a high culture. It must be able to illuminate from a fixed position all its experience; it must bring to full realization the high forms as well as the contradictions and miseries inherent in human society.

The miseries and contradictions bemuse and alarm us

now. I hope I shall not be called flint-hearted if I dare to believe that the humanitarian spirit can never remove them. So long as society is committed to a class-system—and it will probably never be committed to a classless system—the hard-hearted will keep on believing that the high forms are as necessary to the whole of society as bread to the major fraction to whom it is now denied. If man does not live by bread alone, he lives thinly upon bread and sentiment; for sentiment and bread will nourish him but little unless they partake of the peculiarly elevating virtues of form. I might even quote Shelley, whom it is becoming fashionable again to quote: "Our calculations have outrun conception; we have eaten more than we can digest." I am willing to take the sentence in full literalness, if I may read form for conception, and produced for eaten. For the concrete forms of the social and religious life are the assimilating structure of society.

Where, as in the Old South, there were high forms, but no deep realization of the spirit was achieved, we must ask questions. (The right questions: not why the South refused to believe in Progress, or why it did not experiment with "ideas.") Was the structure of society favorable to a great literature? Suppose it to have been favorable: Was there something wrong with the intellectual life that cannot be blamed upon the social order?

The answer is both yes and no to the first question. It is emphatically yes and no to the second. So our answers are confused. At a glance one would expect the rich leisured class, highly educated as the Southern aristocracy was—for the South of the fifties had proportionately a larger educated minority than Massachusetts—to devote a great part of its vitality to the arts, the high and conscious arts. As for the arts otherwise, even peasant societies achieve the less conscious variety—manners, ritual, charming domestic architecture.

Assuming, as I do not think I am allowed to assume very confidently, that this society was a good soil for the high arts, there was yet a grave fault in the intellectual life. It was hag-ridden with politics. We like to think that Archimago sent the nightmare down from the North. He did. But it was partly rooted in the kind of rule that the South had, which was aristocratic rule. All aristocracies are obsessed politically. (Witness *Henry IV*, Parts One and Two; *Henry V*.) The best intellectual energy goes into politics and goes of necessity; aristocracy is class-rule; and the class must fight for interest and power. Under the special conditions of the nineteenth century, the South had less excess of vitality for the disinterested arts of literature than it might have had ordinarily. There are no simple answers to the questions that I have asked. The South was a fairly good place for the arts, as good possibly as any other aristocratic country; only its inherent passion for politics was inflamed by the furious contentions that threatened its life. Every gifted person went into politics, not merely the majority.

The furious contentions themselves provided later answers to the problem of the arts in the South. At the end of the century one of the popular answers was that of the

distinguished William Peterfield Trent, who laid bare all
the Southern defects with the black magic talisman, Slavery. The defects could be whisked away, he argued in his
life of Simms, with "essential faith in American democracy." The Northern people, at that time, may be for-
given this faith; it was the stuffed shirt of plutocracy and
it was making them money; they had a right to believe
in it. I cannot decide between credulity and venality as
the reason for its being believed in the South. I am certain that in Trent's case it was credulity. If slavery was
the cause of war, then slavery explained the political
mania of the Old South; and the political mania stunted
the arts. Partly true; partly false. Such an answer is more
dangerous than an answer wholly false. In this instance
it led the people to believe that their sole obstacle to perfection, slavery, had been removed. There was no need to
be critical of anything else, least of all of the society that
had come down and removed the blight: a society that
by some syllogistic process unknown to me was accepted
as perfect by the new Southern Liberals.

But the abolition of slavery did not make for a distinc-
tively Southern literature. We must seek the cause of our
limitations elsewhere. It is worth remarking, for the sake
of argument, that chattel slavery is not demonstrably a
worse form of slavery than any other upon which an
aristocracy may base its power and wealth. That *African*
chattel slavery was the worst groundwork conceivable for
the growth of a great culture of European pattern, is
scarcely at this day arguable. Still, as a favorable "cultural

situation" it was probably worse than white-chattel, agricultural slavery only in degree. The distance between white master and black slave was unalterably greater than that between white master and white serf after the destruction of feudalism. The peasant *is* the soil. The Negro slave was a barrier between the ruling class and the soil. If we look at aristocracies in Europe, say in eighteenth-century England, we find at least genuine social classes, each carrying on a different level of the common culture. But in the Old South, and under the worse form of slavery that afflicts both races today, genuine social classes do not exist. The enormous "difference" of the Negro doomed him from the beginning to an economic status purely: he has had much the same thinning influence upon the class above him as the anonymous city proletariat has had upon the culture of industrial capitalism.

All great cultures have been rooted in peasantries, in free peasantries, I believe, such as the English yeomanry before the fourteenth century: they have been the growth of the soil. What the Southern system might have accomplished we do not know: it would have been, as I have said, something new. Of course, the absence of genuine cultural capitals in the South has been cited as a cause of lassitude in the arts; perhaps it was a cause, as it is today. But it does not wholly explain the vague and feeble literature that was produced. The white man got nothing from the Negro, no profound image of himself in terms of the soil.

I suspect that, in the age of social science, the term image is not clear, and this, I suppose, is due to the disappearance, in such an age, of the deep relation between man and a local habitation. An environment is an abstraction, not a place; Natchez is a place but not an environment. The difference will be clear to those who are morally able to see that it exists. The citizen of Natchez lived in a place but he could not deepen his sense of its life through the long series of gradations represented by his dependents, who stood between him and the earth. He instructed his factor to buy good furniture of the Second Empire, and remained a Colonial. But the Negro, who has long been described as a responsibility, got everything from the white man. The history of French culture, I suppose, has been quite different. The high arts have been grafted upon the peasant stock. We could graft no new life upon the Negro; he was too different, too alien.

Doubtless the confirmed if genteel romanticism of the old Southern imaginative literature (I make exception for the political writers of South Carolina—Hammond, Harper, Calhoun: they are classical and realistic) was in the general stream of romanticism; yet the special qualities that it produced, the unreal union of formless revery and correct sentiment, the inflated oratory—even in private correspondence you see it witness a feeble hold upon place and time. The roots were not deep enough in the soil. Professor Trent was right; but he was right for the wrong reason. It was not that slavery was corrupt "morally." Societies can bear an amazing amount of corruption and still produce high cultures. Black slavery could not nurture the white man in his own image.

Although the Southern system, in spite of the Negro, was closer to the soil than the mercantile-manufacturing system of the Middle and New England states, its deficiencies in spiritual soil were more serious even than those of the debased feudal society of eighteenth-century rural England. With this society the ante-bellum South had much in common.

The South came from eighteenth-century England, its agricultural half; there were not enough large towns in the South to complete the picture of an England reproduced. The Virginian and the Carolinian, however, imitated the English squire. They held their land, like their British compeer, in absolute, that is to say unfeudal, ownership, as a result of the destruction, first under Henry VIII and then under Cromwell, of the feudal system of land tenure. The landlord might be humane, but he owed no legal obligation to his land (he could wear it out) or to his labor (he could turn it off: called "enclosure" in England, "selling" under Negro slavery). A pure aristocracy, or the benevolent rule of a landed class in the interest of its own wealth and power, had superseded royalty which, in theory at any rate, and often in practice, had tried to balance class interests under protection of the Crown.

It should be borne in mind, against modern egalitarian and Marxian superstition, that royalty and aristocracy are fundamentally opposed systems of rule; that plutocracy, the offspring of democracy, and that Marxism, the child of plutocracy, are essentially of the aristocratic political mode: they all mean class rule. Virginia took the lead in the American Revolution, not to set up democracy, as Jefferson tried to believe, but to increase the power of the tobacco-exporting aristocracy. The planters wished to throw off the yoke of the British merchant and to get access to the free world market.

But the Southern man of letters cannot permit himself to look upon the old system from a purely social point of view, or from the economic view: to him it must seem better than the system that destroyed it, better, too, than any system with which the modern planners, Marxian or other color, wish to replace the present order. Yet the very merits of the Old South tend to confuse the issue: its comparative stability, its realistic limitation of the acquisitive impulse, its preference for human relations compared to relations economic, tempt the historian to defend the poor literature on the mere basis that he feels that the old society was a better place to live in than the new. It is a great temptation—if you do not read the literature.

There is, I believe, a nice object-lesson to be drawn from the changed relation of the English writer to society in the eighteenth century; it is a lesson that bears directly upon the attitude of the Old South towards the profession of letters. In the seventeenth century, in the year 1634, a young, finical man, then in seclusion at

Horton after taking his degrees at Cambridge, and till then unknown, was invited by the Earl of Bridgewater to write a masque for certain revels to be celebrated at Ludlow Castle. The masque was *Comus,* and the revels were in the feudal tradition. The whole celebration was "at home"; it was a part of the community life, the common people were present, and the poet was a spiritual member of the society gathered there. He might not be a gentleman: had Milton become a member of Egerton's "household" he would have been a sort of upper servant. But he would have been a member of the social and spiritual community.

Now examine the affair between Johnson and the Earl of Chesterfield: it is the eighteenth century. It was conducted in the new "aristocratic" style. For the flattery of a dedication the nobleman was loftily willing to give his patronage, a certain amount of money, to an author who had already completed the work, an author who had faced starvation in isolation from society. There is no great publishing system in question here; there were only booksellers. But there was already the cash nexus between the writer and society. The Earl of Chesterfield was a capitalist, not a feudal noble as Egerton to some extent still was: Chesterfield had lost the community; he required of the arts a compliment to the power of his class.

He was the forerunner of the modern plutocrat who thinks that the arts are thriving so long as he can buy Italian paintings, or so long as he creates "foundations" for the arts, or the sales sheets of the publishers show a large volume of "business." But the plutocrat no less than the artist participates in his society through the cash nexus. I hope I do not convince the reader that this wicked fellow has undertaken a deliberate conspiracy against the artist. The artist as man invariably has the same relation to the society of his time as everybody else has: his misfortune and his great value is his superior awareness of that relation. The "message" of modern art at present is that social man is living, without religion, morality, or art, without the high form that reduces all three to an organic whole, in a mere system of money references through which neither artist nor the plutocrat can perform as an entire person.

Is there anything in common between the Earl of Chesterfield and a dour Scots merchant building a fortune and a place in the society of Richmond, Virginia, in the first third of the nineteenth century? I think that they have something in common. It was not John Allan who drove Poe out of Virginia. The foreigner, trying to better himself, always knows the practical instincts of a society more shrewdly than the society knows them. Allan was, for once, the spokesman of Virginia, of the plantation South. There was no place for Poe in the spiritual community of Virginia; there was no class of professional writers that Poe could join in dedicating their works to the aristocracy under the system of the cash nexus. The promising young men were all in politics bent upon more desperate emergencies. It was obvious, even to John Allan, I suppose, that here was no dabbler who would write pleasant, genteel poems and stories for magazines where other dabbling gentlemen printed their pleasant, genteel stories and poems. Anybody could have looked at Poe and known that he meant business.

And until the desperate men today who mean business can become an independent class, there will be no profession of letters anywhere in America. It remains only to add to the brief history adumbrated in this essay some comment on the present situation of the desperate men of the South in particular. There are too many ladies and gentlemen, too many Congreves whose coxcombry a visit from Voltaire would do a great deal of good. I trust that I do not argue the case too well. Congreve frivolously gave up the honor of his profession when Voltaire asked to see the great dramatist and got the answer that Mr. Congreve was no scribbler but a man of fashion. They were more explicit about those things in those days. I should barely hope that the Southern writer, or the Northern or Western, for that matter, may decide that his gentility, being a quality over which he has no control, may get along the best it can. For the genteel tradition has never done anything for letters in the South; yet the Southern writers who are too fastidious to become conscious of their profession have not refused to write best-sellers when they could, and to profit by a cash nexus with New York. I would fain believe that matters are otherwise than so: but facts are facts. If there is such a person as a Southern writer, if there could be such a pro-

fession as letters in the South, the profession would require the speaking of unpleasant words and the violation
of good literary manners.

I wish this were the whole story: only cranks and talents of the quiet, first order maintain themselves against
fashion and prosperity. But even these desperate persons
must live, and they cannot live in the South without an
"independent income." We must respect the source of
our income, that is, we ought to; and if we cannot respect
it we are likely to fear it. This kind of writer is not luck-
ier than his penniless fellow. (The only man I know who
devotes a large income to changing the system that produced it is a New Yorker.) Because there is no city in
the South where writers may gather, write, and live, and
no Southern publisher to print their books, the Southern
writer, of my generation at least, went to New York.
There he was influenced not only by the necessity to live
but by theories and movements drifting over from Europe.

It was, possibly, a dangerous situation. Mr. John Crowe
Ransom has pointed out its implications:

If modernism is regarded as nothing but a new technique, what
was wrong with the old technique? Principally, perhaps, the fact
that it was old; for modernism is apt to assume that tradition is
not so much a prop which may be leant upon as a dead burden
which must be borne. The substance of modernism is not a technique but an attitude. And a dangerous attitude . . .

The Southern artists in going modern offer us their impression
of a general decay, and that is not a pleasant thing to think about.*

* *Modern With a Southern Accent.* By John Crowe Ransom. *The Virginia
Quarterly Review*, April, 1935.

The Southern writer was perilously near to losing his identity, becoming merely a "modern" writer. He lost the Southern feeling which, in the case of Mr. Young, informs the Southern style: he might retain a Southern subject and write about it as an outsider, with some novelty of technique and in smart, superior detachment. These bad features of the last decade may be deplored, I hope, without asking the Southerner to stay at home and starve. That, it seems to me, is what Mr. Ransom asks the Southern writer to do. It was not an uprooted modern, but the classical Milton who remarked, "Wherever we do well is home": wherever we are allowed best to realize our natures—a realization that, for an artist, presupposes permission to follow his craft—is the proper place to live. The Southern writer should if possible be a Southerner in the South. The sole condition that would make that possible is a profession of letters.

But the arts everywhere spring from a mysterious union of indigenous materials and foreign influences: there is no great art or literature that does not bear the marks of this fusion. So I cannot assume, as Mr. Ransom seems to do, that exposure to the world of modernism (Petrarchism was modernism in the England of 1540) was of itself a demoralizing experience. Isn't it rather that the Southerner before he left home had grown weak in his native allegiance? That his political and social history, and his domestic life, had been severely adulterated no less by his fellow Southerners than by the people in the North to whom he fled? Apart from this menace abroad, who cannot bring himself to wish that Miss Glasgow had studied James and Flaubert in her apprenticeship, and spared herself and us her first three or four novels? Could Mr. Young have written his fiction, to say nothing of his plays and criticism, had he read only Cable and Page? And, lastly, what shall we say of Mr. Ransom's own distinguished and very modern poetry?

Is not Mr. Ransom really deploring the absence, as I deplore it, of a professional spirit and professional opportunities in Southern literature? There is no reason why the Southern writer should not address a large public, but if he does he will learn sooner or later that—but for happy accidents—the market, with what the market implies, dictates the style. To create a profession of literature in the South we should require first an independent machinery of publication. I fall into the mechanical terms. A Southern publishing system would not, I imagine, publish Southern books alone; nor should Southern magazines print only Southern authors. The point of the argument leads to no such comforting simplicity. The literary artist is not a successful colonial; he should be able to enjoy the normal belief that he is at the center of the world. One aid to that feeling would be a congenial medium of communication with his public. Let the world in this fashion sit at his feet; let him not have to seek the world.

The exact degree of immediate satisfaction that Southern publication would bring to its authors I cannot predict. It, too, would be the system of the cash nexus; and the Southern publisher would be a capitalist plutocrat not noticeably different from his colleague in the North. Like his Northern friend he would, for a few years at least, sell the Southern article mostly north of the border. Until he could be backed by a powerful Southern press he would need the support of the New York journals for his authors, if he expected them to be read at home. I suppose the benefits of a Southern system would lie chiefly in this: that the Southern writer would not have to run the New York gauntlet, from which he emerges with a good understanding of what he can and cannot do.

We have exchanged the reasoned indifference of aristocracy for the piratical commercialism of plutocracy. Repudiating the later master, the new profession in the South would have to tell New York, where it had hitherto hawked its wares, that no more wares of the prescribed kind would be produced. For the prescribed ware is the ware that the Southerner also must produce, and it is not heartening to observe that his own Southern public waits for the New York journals to prescribe the kind, before he can get a hearing at home. Can there be a profession of letters in the South? Our best critical writing—and we have critical writing of distinction—can never constitute a Southern criticism so long as it must be trimmed and scattered in Northern magazines, or published in books that will be read as curiously as travel literature, by Northern people alone.

The considerable achievement of Southerners in modern American letters must not beguile us into too much hope for the future. The Southern novelist has left his mark upon the age; but it is of the age. From the peculiarly historical consciousness of the Southern writer has come good work of a special order; but the focus of this consciousness is quite temporary. It has made possible the curious burst of intelligence that we get at a crossing of the ways, not unlike, on an infinitesimal scale, the outburst of poetic genius at the end of the sixteenth century when commercial England had already begun to crush feudal England. The Histories and Tragedies of Shakespeare record the death of the old régime, and Doctor Faustus gives up feudal order for world power.

The prevailing economic passion of the age once more tempts, even commands, the Southern writer to go into politics. Our neo-communism is the new form in which the writer from all sections is to be dominated by capitalism, or "economic society." It is the new political mania. And there is no escape from it. The political mind always finds itself in an emergency. And the emergency, this time real enough, becomes a pretext for ignoring the arts. We live in the sort of age that Abraham Cowley complained of—a good age to write about but a hard age to write in.

RELIGION AND THE OLD SOUTH

I

AT one time not inconceivably long ago the ordinary layman, or even the extraordinary one who took up the mysteries as a gentlemanly pursuit, had an impressive respect for the professional man of religion, who for some reason not clear to us had authority to speak of the Higher Things. We have none of that respect now. The present writer, who is a layman of more ordinary kind, is deficient in it. There are priests here and there, a Protestant clergyman or two, who as individuals seem to speak from the tripod. But they hardly represent their class; they are only laymen of the more extraordinary kind. So I begin an essay on religion with almost no humility at all; that is to say, I begin it in a spirit of irreligion. One must think for oneself—a responsibility intolerable to the religious mind, whose proper business is to prepare the mysteries for others.

Religion is not properly a discussion of anything. A discussion of religion is an act of violence, a betrayal of the religious essence undertaken for its own good, or for the good of those who live by it. This is the sole justification of an amateur treatment of religion; my betrayal of religion betrays only my own, and instead of a public scandal it is an instance of personal indecorum that can injure no one but myself.

But there is also a certain pretension in this incivility, and it may as well out. It is to the effect that my private fable was once more public, and that men have fallen away from it into evil days. I must therefore proceed at once to dress my fable in First Principles—which are indeed the only dress it will receive in this essay. I can hardly make a fiction convincing by leaving it in the simple condition that it enjoys in my own mind—that is, the condition of fairy story and myth. For a myth should be in conviction immediate, direct, overwhelming, and I take it that the appreciation of this kind of imagery is an art lost to the modern mind.

The reader must be entreated to follow a few pages of abstraction about religion, but partaking of religion not an ounce. For abstraction is the death of religion no less than the death of everything else.

Religion, when it directs its attention to the horse cropping the blue-grass on the lawn, is concerned with the whole horse, and not with that part of him which he has in common with other horses, or that more general part which he shares with other quadrupeds or with the more general vertebrates; and not with the abstract horse in his capacity of horse-power in general, power that he shares with other machines of making objects move. Religion admits the existence of this horse, but says that he is only half of the horse. Religion offers to place before us the whole horse as he is in himself.

Since this essay is not religion, but a discussion of it, it does not pretend to put before you the complete horse. It does hope to do the following: to show that the complete horse may be there in spite of the impotence of this discussion to produce him. In other words, there is a complete and self-contained horse despite the now prevailing faith that there is none simply because the abstract and scientific mind cannot see him.

This modern mind sees only half of the horse—that half which may become a dynamo, or an automobile, or any other horsepowered machine. If this mind had had much respect for the full-bodied, grass-eating horse, it would never have invented the engine which represents only half of him. The religious mind, on the other hand, has this respect; it wants the whole horse; and it will be satisfied with nothing less.

It wants the whole horse if it is a religious mind that requires more than a half-religion. A religion of the half-horse is pre-eminently a religion concerning how things work, and this is a modern religion. By leaving half of the horse out of account, it can easily show that abstract horsepower, ideally, everywhere, infallibly, under other abstract and *half* conditions, works. Now the half of the animal that this religion leaves out won't work at all; it isn't workable; it is a vast body of concrete qualities constantly conflicting with the workable half; today the horse saddled admirably, but yesterday he ran away—he would not work.

From this it is clear that there is another possible half-religion. It is very common at present. It asserts that nothing works—a poor if desperate refutation of the other half-religion. It says that no horse is workable; the horse is just a locus of unpredictable and immeasurable qualities, and the more you contemplate him the more you see how futile it is to pretend that there is anything regular about him. He is unique beyond cure, and you can't predict the performance of Man o' War tomorrow from the performance of Man o' War yesterday. This is as bad as saying that you can predict everything. It is another half-religion: it is the religion of the symbolist poets and of M. Henri Bergson.

But how do we know that the religion of the completely workable is a religion? It has no altars—that is, no altars that befit it entirely, for it has only usurped the altars traditionally surviving; it has no formal ritual, and no priesthood wearing anything like a cassock or telling anything like beads. We know that the cult of infallible working is a kind of religion because it sets up an irrational value: the value is irrational (a false absolute) because the whole nature of man is not to be subsumed under a concept of logical necessity; the value would still be irrational even if "reason," or science, could reach absolute natural truth. T. E. Hulme would have said that it is contrary to the full content of our experience to assume that man is continuous with nature. It is, then, irrational to believe in omnipotent human rationality. Nothing, in short, infallibly works. The new half-religionists are simply worshipping a principle, and with true half-religious

fanaticism they ignore what they do not want to see—
which is the breakdown of the principle in numerous instances of practice. It is a bad religion, for that very reason; it can predict only success.

The religion, then, of the whole horse predicts both
success and failure. It says that the horse will work within limits, but that it is folly to tempt the horse-providence
too far. It takes account of the failures—that is, it is realistic, for it calls to witness the traditional experience of
evil which is the common lot of the race. It is a mature
religion, and it is not likely to suffer disillusion and collapse. Here it is very unlike the half-religion of work
which has a short memory of failure; the half-religion
can ignore its failures to a certain saturation point, beyond
which they will be overwhelming, and the society living
under it is riding for a crushing fall. It will be totally
unprepared for collapse; it will have gone too far. It will
have forgotten the symbol of itself in the career of the
vaunting Œdipus, who, blind at last, cautioned us not to
pronounce a man happy till we saw the end of his life.
The half-religion of work has accomplished the murder
of Laius and married Jocasta; it has applied its pragmatism of values with astonishing success *up to now;* but
the end is yet to come. Tiresias is yet to come.

Mr. T. S. Eliot meant to show this when he brought
Tiresias into his poem *The Waste Land;* for the seer presents the bankruptcy of the modern program as this program is acted out in that most terrible scene in modern
poetry—the brutally indifferent seduction of the typist

171

by the "small house-agent's clerk." The seduction "works"; it works perfectly, too well. The very working testifies to its failure. It can only be mechanically repeated again and again.

It is apparent that the image of the horse will "work" only in a limited number of illustrations; so I propose to try another image.

II

Take the far more complex image of history, if it may be called an image at all. For as an image its content is mixed and incoherent, and reduces to a vast clutter of particular images. We are able each of us to take our choice; we may reconstruct this scene or that period. We have those people who prefer the Renaissance, and those who like better the Periclean age, or perhaps they concentrate their loyalty to a special kind of life in a particular document of an age or a people: there are Platonists and Aristotelians, Stoics, and Hedonists, and there are the Christians, or at least there were the Christians who stood by the two Testaments, both of which we are now convinced are of ancient and obscure origin and of muddled contents.

These sad, more concrete minds may be said to look at their history in a definite and now quite unfashionable way. They look at it as a concrete series that has taken place in a very real time—by which I mean, without too much definition, a time as sensible, as full of sensation, and as replete with accident and uncertainty as the time they themselves are living in, moment by moment.

But if you do not take history as an image or many images, you have got to take it as idea, abstraction, concept. You need not feel any great interest in the rival merits of the Greek and Roman cultures; they were both "ideas" comprehensible after some study under a single concept which their chief business is now to illustrate. Consider Hegel: it is thesis-antithesis-synthesis—a process that includes not only Greece, Iraq, and Rome, but (as the author warns us about his rights of translation) the Scandinavian as well. It is not that the scientific historian refuses to see that Pericles dressed, ate, and loved differently from Cincinnatus; it is rather that the particular instance fades away into a realm of phenomena related as cause and effect. The historical ideal is the physicist's concept of natural law. There is then ideally no accident of contingency; for accident and contingency are names for our insufficient information. The illusion of contingency that harassed the past (when it was still the present) is dissolved by the Long View—which means that the ancient versions of nature and society were so limited that the ancients were not able to see their pluralism in the true light of all-embracing principle. For this Long View history becomes an abstract series, opposed to the concrete series of the Short View.

There are several questions here that need to be asked of the Long View: Is it not the religion of the half-horse? Does the law of cause and effect which joins up the Greek and Roman cultures make them identical in any other respect than law? Is it, in short, the Greek and Roman cultures themselves? Is it these cultures in any other sense than the merely working horse is the actual horse?

I have said that this view makes the past an abstract series; let it be called a logical series, and there is nothing to do but to resort to the customary *A, B, C* of the text-books. These letters may follow one another at all places at all times, without sensation, accident, or contingency. But did Greek culture live and have its being without sensation? The Short View maintains that it did not, for the Short View holds that the proper series for history to be placed in is the temporal or concrete series.

At this point I must do some violence to the reaches of the argument, and briefly say: for the Short View, history is the specific account of the doings of specific men who acted their parts in a rich and contemporaneous setting which bewildered them. In their bewilderment they invented, or preserved even older, simple stories with a moral. In the times of natural bewilderment—when contingency was called religious awe—men like Hesiod and Cynewulf pondered what they did not understand and gave us simple stories and charms with a moral that we find obvious. But, for the moment, I must leave the moral in a very general state, and close this part of the argument with another difference between the Long and the Short View.

It is apparent that a solvent which reduces the Greek and the Roman cultures to identity of natural law gives to us the privilege of choosing between them; for assuming even that we are the offshoot of one of them, there is yet no reason why we cannot take up the other. The Long View becomes, in brief, the cosmopolitan destroyer of tradition. Or, put otherwise, since the Christian myth is a vegetation rite, varying only in some details from countless other vegetation myths, there is no reason to prefer Christ to Adonis. Varying only in some details: this assumes that there is nothing but a quantitative difference between a horse and a dog, both being vertebrates, mammals, quadrupeds. But the Short View holds that the whole Christ and the whole Adonis are sufficiently differentiated in their respective qualities (details), and that our tradition compels us to choose more than that half of Christ which is Adonis and to take the whole, separate, and unique Christ.

There is a nice and somewhat slippery paradox here: Why should our tradition compel us to choose anything? Particularly in view of the all but accomplished fact that tradition is destroyed? If the agency is shut up, the business cannot be transacted. And we have to confess that merely living in a certain stream of civilized influence does not compel us to be loyal to it. Indeed, the act of loyalty, even the fact of loyalty, must be spontaneous to count at all. Tradition must, in other words, be automatically operative before it can be called tradition. For in its true function it is powerfully selective, and the moment it admits that Adonis is able to compete with Christ, though it regret the rivalry, it has gone over to the Long View; its faith has weakened; and we are on the verge of committing ourselves to the half religions that are no religions at all, but quite simply decisions passed on the utility, the workableness, of the religious objects with respect to the practical aims of society. The utility of the religious object is not impressive.

So this is the paradox: Is it tradition or the Long View itself which prompts the present defense of the religious attitude? It is probably a little of both; though this conception is wholly irrational. It is irrational to defend religion with the weapon that invariably discredits it, and yet this is what seems to be happening. I am trying to discover the place that religion holds, with abstract instruments, which of course tend to put religion into some logical system or series, where it vanishes.

III

But this is due to our nature, which is a very different nature from that of the Russian or eastern European mind, whose religion is quite simply supernaturalism or the naïve religion of the entire horse. It never suspects the existence of those halves that render our sanity so precarious and compel us to vacillate between a self-destroying naturalism and practicality, on the one hand, and a self-destroying mysticism, on the other. For it seems that we are not able to contemplate those qualities of the horse that are specifically religious without forgetting his merely spatial and practicable half: we cannot let the entire horse fill our minds all at once. And thus we have a special notion of tradition—a notion that tradition is not simply a fact, but a fact that must be constantly defended.

This defense is dogma. The strictly qualitative half of the horse, his special uniqueness as a sensible fact, in a word, his image, must be defended against pure practicality, or his abstraction. His defense with us is abstraction itself. For the only defense we know is rational and scientific, and it is thus evident that dogma is not a personal property of religion, but is a mere instrument. And it is an act of sheer generosity when this instrument sets about the defense of its natural enemy, the qualitative view of experience. But, in the Middle Ages, it was so enamoured of this enemy that it could not be brought to destroy him. Yet dogma as rationality is certainly a half-religion and is on the way to becoming science or practicality.

It was both a great discovery and a great calamity when the Europeans found that reason could be used in another way than the defense of something alien to it. It must always seem to us a scandal that Scholasticism should have tried to make rational all those unique qualities of the horse which are spirits and myths and symbols. The men of the Renaissance effectively hushed the scandal up; they said: *Entia non sunt multiplicanda praeter necessitatem.* This razor of William of Occam's at first went only after the superfluous entities of scholastic science. Don't, it says in effect, explain reason in terms of faculties when sub-laryngeal agitation accounts adequately for the phenomena of thought. But it was only a step up from natural phenomena to supernatural noumena, once the razor had become a standard feature of the *Zeitgeist* of the Renaissance. Throw over the spirits and symbols, which are mystical anyhow, not empirically necessary, and find those quantities in nature that will explain, not *what* nature is, but *how* nature works, the quantities that are barely necessary to the working.

This was always the peril of the European mind and the mediæval Church knew it. By making reason, science, or nature, an instrument of defense for the protection of the other than reasonable, the other than scientific, the other than natural, it performed a tremendous feat of spiritual unity. It was the only kind of unity that the Western mind is capable of. Its special feature is the implied belief, which of course became often explicit—I simply mean that the belief, beginning unconsciously in experience, became later necessary as a reasoned part of the system—its special feature is an ineradicable belief in the fundamental evil of nature. Western Reason has always played the ostrich by sticking its head in the Supernatural. Woe betide when it took its head out and got so used to the natural setting that it found it good. And this is what happened. For the Church had known that the only way to restrain the practical impulses of her constituency was to put into the mouth of nature the words *Noli me tangere.* The Eastern Church never had to do this, nor did it ever have to construct a plausible rationality round the supernatural to make it acceptable; it has never had a philosophy, nor a dogma in our sense; it never needed one.

The Western Church established a system of quantity for the protection of quality, but there was always the danger that quantity would revolt from servitude and suppress its master; the danger that it would apply its genius to a field more favorable to spectacular success. Once reason ceased to be the instrument through which the purely qualitative features of nature could be contemplated and enjoyed, without being corrupted by too much use, it began to see the natural setting as so many instances of quantity; that is, nature began to see the practical possibilities of knowing herself. For reason and nature are one, and that is the meaning of naturalism. The symbol and the myth meant that the external world was largely an inviolable whole; once the symbol and the myth were proved to be not natural facts, but unnatural fictions that fitted into no logical series tolerable to the rational mind, nature became simply a workable half. The votaries of this nature now think that it is a Whole of limitless practicability.

IV

This being true, how can tradition, which is always embarrassing to practicality on a large scale, be defended? Has it not disappeared? And was it not always on the brink of compromise in the fact that it needed the support of its enemy? The answer doubtless is: It can always be defended, but a recovery and restoration is a more difficult performance.

Moreover, where can an American take hold of tradition? His country is supposed to have preserved none from Europe, and if we take the prototype of the European tradition to be mediæval society, we must confess that America has performed wonders, considering her youth, in breaking it down.

Yet the very idea "America" must give us pause, for it is almost anything that a determined apologist may wish to represent. In a brief three hundred years she has recapitulated practically every form of European polity, if these separate polities may be seen as devoid of their religious background. She has repeated all the chief economic and political forms. But she has not repeated the religious forms. The religious history of America is perfectly continuous with that of Europe.

This anomaly gave us that remarkable society of the old South, which was a feudal society, without a feudal religion; hence only a semi-feudal society. The reason for this is by no means obscure. It is just possible to see the Jamestown project as the symbol of what later happened to America: it was a capitalistic enterprise undertaken by Europeans who were already convinced adherents of large-scale exploitation of nature, not to support a stable religious order, but to advance the interests of *trade as an end in itself*. They stood thus for a certain stage in the disintegration of the European religion, and their descendants stuck to their guns, which theoretically at least were Protestant, aggressive, and materialistic guns.

At the same time certain conditions of economy supported a society which was, again theoretically, Protestant, but which was not aggressive and materialistic. It was a throw-back, a case of atavism. A distinguished Southern writer has argued that the Southern population was originally less rebellious against European stability than was the Northern. It is doubtful if history will support this, though I should personally like to do so, for the belief implies the myth-making tendency of the mind in one of its most valuable forms. The enemy, abstraction, or the view of history as the logical series, gives us, alas, another story. It is that soil and climate made the agrarian life generally more attractive than a barrener soil and a colder climate could have ever done, and that the propitious soil and climate made it possible for a semi-feudal system of labor to take root and thrive. A people may, in short, return to an older economy, under certain local conditions; but international conditions, certainly since the sixteenth century, have made it impossible for any community of European origin to remain spiritually isolated and to develop its genius, unless that genius is in harmony with the religious and economic drift of the civilization at large.

The South could temporarily return to an older secular polity, but the world was too much with it, and it could not create its appropriate religion.

There were two results of this anomalous position that may be stated without too much historical argument. The South, as a political atmosphere charged with eighteenth-century ideas, did not realize her genius in time. She consistently defended herself with the political terms of eighteenth-century liberalism, a doctrine better suited to the middle-class economics of the North, into whose hands she neatly played. So, waiting too long, she let her more powerful rival gain the ascendancy. The South did not achieve that inward conviction of destiny that empowers societies no less than individuals to understand their position and to act from inner necessity: we do nothing without symbols and we cannot do the right thing with the wrong symbol. There was no unity of purpose between the Southern Protestant religion and the Southern Protestant semi-feudalism. The South's religious mind was inarticulate, dissenting, and schismatical. She had a non-agrarian and trading religion that had been invented in the sixteenth century by a young finance-capitalist economy: hardly a religion at all but rather a disguised secular ambition. The Southern politicians quoted scripture to defend slavery, yet they defended their society as a whole with the catchwords of eighteenth-century politics. And this is why the South separated from the North too late, and so lost her cause.

The second result of the anomalous structure of the Southern mind is a near and contemporary one. Because the South never created a fitting religion, the social structure of the South began grievously to break down two generations after the Civil War. For the social structure depends on the economic structure, and economic conviction is still, in spite of the beliefs of economists from Adam Smith to Marx, the secular image of religion. No nation is ever simply and unequivocally beaten in war;

nor was the South. Is it possible that the South shows signs of defeat? If she does, it is due to her lack of a religion which would make her special way of life the inevitable and permanently valuable one. We have been inferior to the Irish in this virtue, though much less than the Irish have we ever been beaten in war.

It appears that the question put at the beginning of this section, How can the American, or the Southern man, take hold of tradition, is further from being answered than ever.

V

Let us return to the two ways of looking at horses and history. Which are we permitted to say was the way of the Old South? The answer to this question is not necessarily disconcerting, even if we must admit both ways. And it is bound to be both because the South was a Western community, and a Western community is one that does not live in sackcloth and ashes and erect all its temples to the gods. The Southerners were capable of using their horses, as they did one day at Brandy Station, but they could also contemplate them as absolute and inviolable objects; they were virtually incapable of abstracting from the horse his horsepower, or from history its historicity. For the horse fact and the historical fact, by remaining concrete, retained a certain status as *images,* and images are only to be contemplated, and perhaps the act of contemplation after long exercise initiates a habit of restraint, and the setting up of absolute standards which are less formulas for action than an interior discipline of the mind. There is doubtless from the viewpoint of abstract history not much difference between a centaur, since we speak of horses, and a Christ, since we speak of historicity. Both are mythical figments reducible in one set of properties to the abstraction man-ness. But the Short View, as we have seen, is incorrigibly selective, and has been known to prefer Christ to the man horse.

After about 1820, in America, the Southern communities alone stood for that preference with anything like a single mind. The heresy of New England is beautifully recorded in the correspondence of John Adams and Thomas Jefferson, where the two sages discuss the possibility of morals. Jefferson calls his judgment "taste"—reliance on custom, breeding, ingrained moral decision. But Adams needs a "process of moral reasoning," which forces the individual to think out from abstract principle his rôle at a critical moment of action. The view of John Adams tells us how far New England had gone from Europe, how deeply she had broken with the past.

While the South in the nineteenth century trafficked with Europe in cotton, she took in exchange very little of manners, literature, or the arts. The Southerners were another community on the complete European plan, and they had no need, being independent, of importing foreign art and noblemen, commodities that New England became frantic about after 1830. For New England was one of those abstract-minded, sharp-witted, trading societies that must be parasites in two ways: they must live economically on some agrarian class or country, and they must live spiritually likewise. New England lived economically on the South, culturally on England. And this was doubtless a disguised and involved nostalgia for the land—the New England "land" being old England. The houses and the universities of New England became a European museum, stuffed with the dead symbols of what the New Englander could not create because provision for it had been left out of his original foundation.

In the nineteenth century New England confessed her loss of the past by being too much interested in Europe. If you take the Adams family at its best, you find a token of the whole New England mind: there is the tragedy of the "Education of Henry Adams," who never quite understood what he was looking for. He spent much of his youth, like Henry James, learning the amenities of the English agrarians, without being by right of soil entitled to them, and never suspecting that the best he might hope to do was to learn them by rote. More significantly he passed his last days in Washington despising the "ignorant" and "simple" minds south of the Potomac, again never suspecting that his efforts in behalf of defeating this simplicity and ignorance in a recent war did something towards undermining the base of the civilized values that he coveted most.

If New England's break with Europe made her excessively interested in the European surface, the ignorance and simplicity of the South's independence of Europe, in the cultural sense, witness a fact of great significance.

The South could be ignorant of Europe because she *was* Europe; that is to say, the South was trying to take root in a native soil. And the South could remain simple-minded because she had no use for the intellectual agility required to define its position. Her position, alas, seemed to be self-sufficient and self-evident; it was European where the New England position was self-conscious and colonial. The Southern mind was simple, not top-heavy with learning it had no need of, unintellectual, and composed; it was personal and dramatic, rather than abstract and metaphysical; and it was sensuous because it lived close to a natural scene of great variety and interest.

Because she lived by images not highly organized, it is true, as dogma, but rather more loosely gathered from the past, the South was a traditional European community. The Southerners were incurable in their preference for Cato over the social conditions in which he historically lived. They looked at history as the concrete and temporal series—a series at all only because they required a straight metaphorical line back into the past, for the series, such as it was, was very capricious, and could hardly boast of a natural logic. They could add to the classics a lively mediævalism from the novels of Sir Walter Scott. They saw themselves as human beings living by a human principle, from which they were unwilling to subtract the human so as to set the principle free to operate on an unlimited program of inhuman practicality. For that is what a principle is—the way things will work. But the Southerner, or more generally the die-hard agrarian, was not willing to let the principle proceed alone, uncontrolled; for what he valued most in the working of principle was the capacity that he retained of enjoying the fruits of the work. The old Southerners were highly critical of the kinds of work to be done. They planted no corn, they grew no cotton that did not directly contribute to the upkeep of a rich private life; and they knew little history for the sake of knowing it, but simply for the sake of contemplating it and seeing in it an image of themselves. It is probable that they liked Plutarch better than Suetonius, and both better than Thucydides. Like all unscientific societies they cared little for natural knowledge, and cared more for that unnaturalism which is morals. They liked very simple stories with a moral in which again they could see an image of themselves.

We have already considered some of the possible reasons why they broke down.

VI

They had a religious life, but it was not enough organized with a right mythology. In fact, their rational life was not powerfully united to the religious experience, as it was in mediæval society, and they are a fine specimen of the tragic pitfall upon which the Western mind has always hovered. Not having a rational system for the defense of their religious attitude and its base in a feudal society, they elaborated no rational system whatever, no full-grown philosophy; so that, when the postbellum temptations of the devil, who, according to Milton and Æschylus, is the exploiter of nature, confronted them, they had no defense. Since there is, in the Western mind, a radical division between the religious, the contemplative, the qualitative, on the one hand, and the scientific, the natural, the practical, on the other, the scientific mind always plays havoc with the spiritual life when it is not powerfully enlisted in its cause; it cannot be permitted to operate alone.

It operated separately (yet along with other ideas that ignored it and one another) in Thomas Jefferson, and the form that it took in his mind may be reduced to a formula: *The ends of man are sufficiently contained in his political destiny*. Now the political destiny of men is the way they work, toward ends they hope to achieve in community by the operation of secular laws. It is not necessary to labor the point, or to draw out the enormous varieties that such a theory may exhibit. It is sufficient to point out that the ante-bellum Southerners never profoundly believed it. It is highly illuminating to reflect that, as I have said, *they acted as if they did*. There was, of course, a good deal of dissent: the Virginia Constitutional Convention repudiated Jefferson in 1832. It was a first step; but the last step was so far off that it could not possibly have preceded 1861.

The modern Southerner inherits the Jeffersonian formula. This is only to say that he inherits a concrete and very unsatisfactory history. He can almost wish for his ease the Northern contempt for his kind of history; he would like to believe that history is not a vast body of concrete fact to which he must be loyal, but only a source of mechanical formulas; for then he might hope to do what the Northern industrialist has just about succeeded in doing—making a society out of abstractions. The Southerner would conjure up some magic abstraction to spirit back to him his very concrete way of life. He would, in short, in his plight, apply the formula, because he has no other, of his inheritance—that the ends of man may be fully achieved by political means.

The South would not have been defeated had she possessed a sufficient faith in her own kind of God. She would not have been defeated, in other words, had she been able to bring out a body of doctrine setting forth her true conviction that the ends of man require more for their realization than politics. The setback of the war was of itself a very trivial one.

We are very near an answer to our question—How may the Southerner take hold of his tradition?

The answer is: by violence.

For this answer, if we want an answer, is inevitable. He cannot fall back upon his religion, simply because it was never articulated and organized for him. If he could do this, he would constitute himself a "borer from within," and might hope to effect gradually a secular revolution in his favor. As we have said, economy is the secular image of religious conviction. His religious conviction is inchoate and unorganized; it never had the opportunity to be anything else.

Since he cannot bore from within, he has remaining

the sole alternative of boring from without. This method is political, active, and, in the nature of the case, violent and revolutionary. Reaction is the most radical of programs; it aims at cutting away the overgrowth and getting back to the roots. A forward-looking radicalism is a contradiction; it aims at rearranging the foliage.

The Southerner is faced with this paradox: He must use an instrument, which is political, and so unrealistic and pretentious that he cannot believe in it, to re-establish a private, self-contained, and essentially spiritual life. I say that he must do this; but that remains to be seen.

REVIEWS

EDWIN ARLINGTON ROBINSON

EDWIN ARLINGTON ROBINSON, most famous
of living American poets, was born at Head Tide,
Maine, on December 22, 1869.* He attended Harvard
from 1891 to 1893, but left college without taking a degree. In 1896 he printed privately his first book of verse,
The Torrent and the Night Before, which was followed
a year later by *The Children of the Night,* a volume little
noticed at the time but one which marks the beginning
of a new era in American poetry. In the next fourteen
years he published two more books, *Captain Craig* (1902)
and *The Town Down the River* (1910). But it was not
until 1916 that he attracted wide attention and won a
notable fame. For with *The Man Against the Sky* Mr.
Robinson stepped quickly into the front rank of American poetry. In his early years he wrote some of the finest
lyrics of modern times: these are likely to be his permanent claim to fame.

Able critics have thought otherwise. Not only, they say,
are Mr. Robinson's long narrative poems his best work;
they are the perfect realization of a "tragic vision." But
hear Mr. Mark Van Doren, a distinguished critic whom I
do not like to disagree with:

His vision is essentially tragic in that it stresses the degeneration of ideas, the dimming of the light, when these become im-

* After this paper had been prepared for the press, Mr. Robinson died of
a lingering illness on April 5, 1935.

plicated in the rough action of the world. (*Edward Arlington Robinson*, p. 34.)

Passion has its victories no less than reason. The tragic picture would be incomplete without either of these. It is because Mr. Robinson's picture is fairly complete that he deserves the rare title of major American poet. (*Ibid.*, p. 90.)

I should be the last person, I hope, to dispute Mr. Robinson's right to that title. Nor should I contend for a moment that Mr. Robinson lacks the "tragic vision," but I am convinced that Mr. Van Doren's qualifying word, *essentially,* is accurate. For Mr. Robinson writes, I believe, less from the tragic vision than from the tragic sentiment; and the result is the pathetic tale of obscure ambition or thwarted passion; not tragedy.

It is true that he deals with the degeneration of ideas. The question that Mr. Van Doren does not ask, it seems to me, is this: what is the exact significance of the ideas? Is their ultimate reference to a religious or philosophical background, a realm of ideas possessing at least for their time and place the compulsion of absolute truth? Or are they the private ideas of modern persons, the personal forms of some egoistic thrust of the will? In other words, is Mr. Robinson a true tragic poet, or is he a modern poet like other modern poets, whose distinguished gifts are not enough to give him more than the romantic ego with which to work?

*Talifer** is a psychological narrative of the order of *The Man Against the Sky*. It is the eighth or ninth specimen

* *Talifer*. By Edwin Arlington Robinson. New York: The Macmillan Co., 1932.

194

of this kind of poem that Mr. Robinson has given us. Because the type has grown thinner with each example, the new narrative being, I believe, the least satisfactory of them all, it is the occasion of some inquiry into the causes of Mr. Robinson's preference for this particular form. It is a form that includes the three Arthurian poems, *Merlin, Lancelot,* and *Tristram,* psychological stories that are in all respects similar to the New England tales of Nightingale, Cavender, Bartholow. All is the same but time and place; for the characters are the same.

In *Talifer* there are four characters, two men and two women. The woman Althea—the name is a dry piece of irony—is in love with Talifer; she is woman domestic, sensitive, but commonplace and child-bearing. Talifer himself is an ordinary person, but he talks of his "tradition," carries himself well, and expects of life more than his inner quality entitles him to: so he imagines that he is in love with the other woman, Karen, who is beautiful, treacherous, cold, and erudite, dividing her time between inscrutable moods and incredible reading in the ancients. But she is vaguely conceived by the poet, and the motivation of the hero's action remains obscure.

Talifer has been fatuous enough to say that with Karen he expects to find Peace. Life becomes, after a year or two with her, intolerable. Then, one day in his ancestral forest, he meets Althea, who still loves him, and he decides to leave Karen. Now all this time, the other man, Doctor Quick, could have been in love with either of the women; he is too skeptical to push his desires; and his place in the story is that of commentator. He explains the confusion to the other characters, and affords to the poet a device by which the real actors become articulate. The story ends with the reappearance, after a couple of years, of Quick: in the meantime Talifer has married Althea, who has by him a child. Although Quick himself has tried to participate in life by taking Karen off to a "cottage in Wales," his return witnesses his failure. But he is not much affected by it. He proceeds to analyze for Althea and Talifer the true basis of their love, which is thoroughly commonplace after a good deal of romantic pretense.

Mr. Robinson's style in the new poem is uniform with the style of its predecessors; it is neither better nor worse than the style of *The Glory of the Nightingales* or of *Cavender's House*. It requires constant reviewing by Mr. Robinson's admirers to keep these poems distinct; at a distance they lose outline; blur into one another. They constitute a single complete poem that the poet has not succeeded in writing, a poem of which these indistinct narratives are partial formulations.

We get, in them all, a character doomed to defeat, or a character who, when the tale opens, is a failure in the eyes of his town, but who wins a secret moral victory, as in *The Man Who Died Twice*. But Talifer, whose ego betrays him into an emotional life that he cannot understand, is not quite defeated. The tragic solution of his problem being thus rejected by Mr. Robinson, and replaced by a somewhat awkward bit of domestic irony,

Talifer at first sight appears to be a new kind of Robinsonian character. Yet the novelty, I think, lies in the appearance. For Talifer is the standard Robinsonian character grown weary of the tragic sentiment, accepting at last the fact that his tilt at fate had less intensity than he supposed, and

> with grateful ears
> That were attuned again to pleasant music
> Heard nothing but the mellow bells of peace.

That is the Tennysonian end of the poem.

I have remarked that the character of Karen is vaguely conceived, with the result that Talifer's relation to her is incomprehensible. Those mellow bells of peace are therefore a little hollow in sound, for their ring is as inexplicable as the noisy chaos of the erudite Karen, upon whose prior significance they entirely depend. The plot, in brief, lacks internal necessity. And the domestic peace of the conclusion remains arbitrary, in spite of Mr. Robinson's efforts through his mouthpiece, Doctor Quick, to point it up with some sly irony at the end. The irony is external—as if Mr. Robinson had not been able to tell the story for what it was, and had to say: This is what life is really like, a simple wife and a child—while ring those bells of peace that would be romantically tiresome if one had tragic dignity.

Mr. Robinson's genius is primarily lyrical; that is to say, he seldom achieves a success in a poem where the idea exceeds the span of a single emotion. It is, I think, significant that in his magnificent *The Mill* the tragic reference sustains the emotion of the poem: his narrative verse yields but a few moments of drama that are swiftly dispersed by the dry casuistry of the commentary upon them. The early *Richard Cory* is a perfect specimen of Mr. Robinson's dramatic powers—when those powers are lyrically expressed; similarly *Luke Havergal*, a poem in which the hard images glow in a fierce intensity of light, is one of the great lyrics of modern times:

> No, there is not a dawn in eastern skies
> To rift the fiery night that's in your eyes;
> But there, where western glooms are gathering
> The dark will end the dark, if anything . . .

Mr. Van Doren is the first critic to appreciate this peculiarly Robinsonian legerdemain with figures of light.

It is probable that the explanation of the popular success of *Tristram*, and of most of Mr. Robinson's narratives, lies in the loss of the dramatic instinct by the contemporary public. It is a loss increasingly great since the rise of middle-class comedy in the eighteenth century. Since then, in the serious play, instead of the tragic hero whose downfall is deeply involved with his suprahuman relations, we get the romantic, sentimental hero whose problem is chiefly one of adjustment to society, on the one hand, and, on the other, one of futile self-assertion in the realm of the personal ego. Mr. Robinson's Talifer exhibits both these phases of the modern sensibility: he plays with his ego in the irrational marriage with Karen, and he later sees his difficulty strictly in terms of a social institution, or of social adjustment, in the marriage with Althea, who, of course, represents "truth."

The dramatic treatment of the situation Mr. Robinson permits himself to neglect; for the dramatic approach would have demanded the possession, by the hero, of a comprehensive moral scheme. He would have applied the scheme with perfect rigor to his total conduct, with the result that it would have broken down somewhere and thrown the hero into a tragic dilemma, from which it had been impossible for him to escape. The story as it is told is hardly more than anecdotal; Mr. Robinson turns his plot, at the end, into an easy joke about the deliquescent effects of marriage upon the pretensions of human nature.

It is one of the anomalies of contemporary literature that Mr. Robinson, who has given us a score of great lyrics, should continue to produce these long narrative poems, one after another, until the reader can scarcely tell them apart. We may only guess the reason for this. Our age provides for the poet no epos or myth, no pattern of well-understood behavior, which the poet may examine in the strong light of his own experience. For it is chiefly those times that prefer one kind of conduct to another, times that offer to the poet a seasoned code, which have produced the greatest dramatic literature. Drama depends for clarity and form upon the existence of such a code. It matters little whether it is a code for the realization of good, like Antigone's; or a code for evil like Macbeth's. The important thing is that it shall tell the poet how people try to behave, and that it shall be too perfect, whether in good or in evil, for human nature. The poet seizes one set of terms within the code —for example, feudal ambition in Macbeth—and shows that the hero's faulty application of the perfect code to his own conduct is doomed to failure. By adhering strictly to the code, the poet exhibits a typical action. The tension between the code and the hero makes the action also specific, unique; the code is at once broken up and affirmed, the hero's resistance at once clarified and defined by the limits thus set to his conduct. Macbeth asserts his ego in terms of the code before him, not in terms of courtly love or of the idealism of the age of Werther: he has no choice of code. The modern character has the liberty of indefinite choice, but not the good fortune to be chosen, as Macbeth and Antigone had.

Mr. Robinson has no epos, myth, or code, no suprahuman truth, to tell him what the terminal points of human conduct are, in this age; so he goes over the same ground, again and again, writing a poem that will not be written.

It has been said by T. S. Eliot that the best lyric poetry of our time is dramatic, that it is good because it is dramatic. It is at least a tenable notion that the dramatic instinct, after the Restoration and down to our own time, survived best in the lyric poets. With the disappearance of general patterns of conduct, the power to depict action that is both single and complete also disappears. The dramatic genius of the poet is held to short flights, and the dramatic lyric is a fragment of a total action which the poet lacks the means to delineate.

It is to be hoped that Mr. Robinson will again exercise his dramatic genius where it has a chance for success: in lyrics. Meanwhile it would be no less disastrous to Mr. Robinson's later fame than to our critical standards, should we admire him too abjectly to examine him. Let him then escape the indignity of Hardy's later years when such a piece of bad verse as *Any Little Old Song* won egregious applause all over the British Isles. That Mr. Robinson is unable to write badly will not excuse us to posterity.

1932

MacLEISH'S CONQUISTADOR*

MR. MacLEISH has been up to this time a poet like most of his contemporaries, limited to the short flight. There is, in his earlier work, no premonitory sounding of the finely sustained tone of *Conquistador* For modern poetry the poem is long. It is an epic in miniature of about two thousand lines. In versification and style, and with respect to the narrational "point of view," there is no other poem in English with which as a whole it may be compared. It is evident, of course, that MacLeish has studied Ezra Pound; but this is no disparagement of Pound's pupil. The *Cantos* are full of technical instruction for the poet who knows what he needs to learn. The followers of Eliot take his "philosophy" as well as his style, and give us work of "lower intensity" than the original. Pound's disciples are either less plausible or more independent. They exercise thinly with Mr. Dudley Fitts or practice the admirable craft of *Conquistador*.

The background of the poem is the conquest of Mexico. For a complete history of the conquest one will have to go to the historians. The poem is a reconstruction of the part played by one of the lesser heroes, Bernal Diaz del Castillo, who as an old man wrote his own story in re-

* *Conquistador.* By Archibald MacLeish. Boston: Houghton-Mifflin Company, 1932.

sentment against the official histories by Gomara and others—

> The quilled professors: the taught tongues of fame:
> What have they written of us: the poor soldiers . . .
>
> They call the towns for the kings that bear no scars:
> They keep the names of the great for time to stare at—
> The bishops rich men generals cocks-at-arms . . .

Bernal tells the story himself, in flashes of recollection that have just enough narrative progression to give to the narrator a constantly new field of imagery. But the historical pattern of the conquest is never explicit, never obtrusive enough to take the reader's attention from the personality of Bernal and the quality of his character. For the personality of Bernal is the subject of the poem.

Thus narrowing the action down to the focus of a single mind and what it saw, MacLeish disposes of two enormous difficulties of epic poetry: he eliminates the objective detail of the total scene, at once the conventional privilege and the burden of the classical poet; and he dispenses with the need of cosmic machinery. There is no external "idea"; there is no theme; there is no "typical action."

We get the peculiarly modern situation: the personality of one man is dramatized against an historical setting. "What have they written of us: the poor soldiers"—what can the private sensibility get out of history to sustain it? What can Bernal get out of his past? Nothing appears in the story that Bernal did not see; it is all enriched by memory. Although Bernal announces his subject as "That which I have myself seen and the fighting," there is little fighting; there is little action; for the dramatic tension of the poem grows out of the narrator-hero's fear of death upon the gradual disappearance of sensation. The dramatic quality of the poem—a quality that has little to do with the story as such—lies thus in the hero's anxiety to recover his sensuous early years, upon which his identity as a person, and hence his life, depends.

This is the subject of the poem. The "meaning" of the poem is an implicit quality of Bernal's mind, but only a modicum of logical violence will isolate it. It is the futility of individual action. For unless the hero, in his old age, can recapture the sensation of action, the very action itself must fade into the obscure shuffle of abstract history. We have seen that Bernal cannot accept the public versions of the conquest. (Is Bernal, then, a soldier of the sixteenth century or of the World War?) He cannot identify the moment of action with the ostensible common purpose for which the whole series of events took place. He is confined to memories, to the mechanism of sensation.

I dwell upon this "meaning" of *Conquistador* for two reasons. It obviously, in the first place, explains the form in which MacLeish found it necessary to cast his narrative, a form that I have briefly described; the necessity of this form explains the presence, I believe, of those features of the style that MacLeish borrowed from Pound and perfected. And, secondly, the meaning of this dis-

tinguished poem, as I apprehend it, may lead some of the
younger critics to reconsider, not their enthusiasm for the
workmanship, which it richly deserves, but their hasty
acceptance of its "philosophy." It is a mistake to suppose
that MacLeish has offered a "way out" of the introspective indecision of the school of T. S. Eliot, affirming a
faith in heroic action against the moral paralysis presumably suffered by the best minds of that older generation. Not only is there, in the poem, a lack of belief in
any kind of action that we might imitate; the poet does
not evince much interest in the action implied by the
reminiscences that support the narrative.

There is not one moment of action rendered objectively
in the entire poem. There is constantly and solely the pattern of sensation that surrounded the moment of action
—the fringe of the physical shock and awareness that survive in memory. The technique of rendering this special
quality of memory is MacLeish's contribution to poetic
style:

Gold there on that shore on the evening sand—
"Colua" they said: pointing on toward the sunset:
They made a sign on the air with their solemn hands . . .

And that voyage it was we came to the Island:
Well I remember the shore and the sound of that place
And the smoke smell on the dunes and the wind dying.

Well I remember the walls and the rusty taste of the
New-spilled blood in the air: many among us
Seeing the priests with their small arrogant faces . . .

205

Ah how the throat of a girl and girl's arms are
Bright in the riding sun and the young sky
And the green year of our lives where the willows are!

This clarity of sensuous reminiscence that suffuses the poem is a new quality in American verse. The images are not imbedded in metaphor; they exist spatially in the round. Pound supplied the model:

Eyes brown topaz,
Brookwater over brown sand,
The white hounds on the slope,
Glide of water, lights on the prore,
Silver beaks out of night,
Stone, bough over bough, lamps fluid in water,
Pine by the black trunk of its shadow
The trees melted in air.

The images are impersonal, objective, and timeless, detached from Pound's moral position. The focus of MacLeish's imagery is personal: the image exists in terms of Bernal's mechanism of memory, of his struggle for personal identity. Its precision has been disciplined in the workshop of Ezra Pound, whose quality of floating clarity is localized by MacLeish in a Browningesque monologue, where the casuistry gives way to a sophisticated version of the *chanson de geste*.

Poets in this age cannot set forth with security a conscious philosophical system. Reasons for this I have mentioned in another place. When there is no systematic philosophy at hand, the poet is likely to slip into an unsystematic one of his own: this, perhaps, is better than an elaborate system that he cannot assimilate and understand. MacLeish's philosophy is personal and unarticulated. It may be stated in moral terms. We cannot linger over even the finest passages of *Conquistador* without becoming aware that we are in the presence of a sentimental view of experience. I have said that there is no objective design to uphold the sensibility of the narrator-hero. Perhaps, in this poem, MacLeish is no less able a poet than the young Milton of *Lycidas;* but Milton had an objective convention that absorbed every implication of his personal feeling. I use the term sentimental, then, in a strict, not a pejorative, sense. The melancholy of the hero's disgust with the "taught tongues of fame" is personal, sentimental; it is necessarily meaningless and obscure.

The disgust of Bernal does not rise to the level of rational criticism. It would serve as a rational evaluation of the "conquest" if there were a full stream of objective action in the light of which it could acquire significance. To have set off the private experience of the soldier against the grandiose avowals of purpose by the conquerors, might possibly have given to the poet the situation of tragic irony. But there is no conflict of this order in the poem. The emotion is pathos. We get Bernal's sentimental regret; his anger rises at the failure of the official historians to recreate the sensuous correspondence to his own part in the campaign. He says in effect not *quorum pars magna fui* but rather *solus quorum omnis fui*—alone in his perceptions. The poem recovers the perceptions but it does not place them against a coherent stream of events. The hero is concerned with his personal survival. He is modern and sentimental; not tragic and ironic. The motivation of his story is the fear of death.

I am ungrateful to MacLeish; I have dwelt upon a philosophical limitation that is not peculiar to this poet, but is deeply rooted in the age. The technical perfection of *Conquistador* is, of course, not merely a technical feat. The poem is one of the examples of our modern sensibility at its best; it has the defect of its qualities.

The verse is *terza rima,* a metrical form enormously difficult in English. The paucity of English rhymes leaves it clumsy and monotonous in all but the hands of a master. Shelley tried it once with moderate success; Wyat adapted it to an epistolary style that doubtless should have been but never was a model for later poets. But MacLeish, foreseeing in a long poem the monotony of conventionally rhymed *terza rima,* varies rhyme with terminal assonance that is usually hidden and always cunningly placed. He achieves something of the fluent ease of the Italian, which is rich in rhyme-words, and gives us the first successful example of *terza rima* in a long English poem.

It is the only considerable metrical achievement by a poet of this generation. Yet the perfection of the experiment will make future use of *terza rima* dangerous. The technique of the verse is a quality of MacLeish's mind, and is inimitable. "Waller refined our numbers"—but this time Waller is a hard-pressed modern whose brilliance, once flashed, burns out before it can be passed to other hands. It is the present fate of poetry to be always beginning over again. The kind of "culture" in *Conquistador* is purely literary; the kind of experience in it is the sentimentality of moral isolation. The refinement of the craftsmanship hovers over a void.

1932

T. S. ELIOT

EVERY age, as it sees itself, is peculiarly distracted: its chroniclers notoriously make too much of the variety before their own eyes. We see the variety of the past as mere turbulence within a fixed unity, and our own uniformity of the surface as the sign of a profound disunity of impulse. We have discovered that the ideas that men lived by from about the twelfth to the seventeenth century were absolute and unquestioned. The social turmoil of European history was shortsighted disagreement as to the best ways of making these deep assumptions morally good.

Although writers were judged morally, poets purveyed ready-made moralities, and no critic expected the poet to give him a brand-new system. A poem was a piece of enjoyment for minds mature enough—that is, convinced enough of a satisfactory destiny—not to demand of every scribbler a way of life.

It is beyond the scope of this discussion, and of my own competence, to attempt an appraisal of any of the more common guides to salvation, including the uncommon one of the Thirty-nine Articles, lately subscribed to by Mr. T. S. Eliot, whose six poems published under the title *Ash Wednesday** are the occasion of this review. For it is my thesis that, in a discussion of Eliot's poetry, his religious doctrines in themselves have little that commands interest. Yet it appears that his poetry, notwith-

* *Ash Wednesday.* By T. S. Eliot. New York: The Fountain Press, 1931.

standing the amount of space it gets in critical journals, receives less discussion each year. The moral and religious attitude implicit in it has been related to the Thirty-nine Articles, and to a general intellectual position that Eliot has defended in his essays. The poetry and the prose are taken together as evidence that the author has made an inefficient adaptation to the modern environment; or at least he doesn't say anything very helpful to the American critics in their struggles to adapt themselves. It is an astonishing fact that, near as we are to a decade obsessed by "æsthetic standards," there is less discussion of poetry in a typical modern essay on that fine art than there is in Johnson's essay on Denham. Johnson's judgment is frankly moralistic; he is revolted by unsound morals; but he seldom capitulates to a moral sentiment because it flatters his own moral sense. He requires the qualities of generality, copiousness, perspicuity. He hates Milton for a regicide. But his judgment of *Paradise Lost* is as disinterested as any judgment we should find today; certainly no more bound by historical prejudice than Mr. Eliot's own views of Milton. Yet Eliot's critics are a little less able each year to see the poetry for Westminster Abbey; the wood is all trees.

I do not pretend to know how far our social and philosophical needs justify a prejudice which may be put somewhat summarily as follows: all forms of human action, economics, politics, even poetry, and certainly industry, are legitimate modes of salvation, but the historic religious mode is illegitimate. It is sufficient here to point out that the man who expects to find salvation in the latest lyric or a well-managed factory will not only not find it there; he is not likely to find it anywhere else. If a young mind is incapable of moral philosophy, a mind without moral philosophy is incapable of understanding poetry. For poetry, of all the arts, demands a serenity of view and a settled temper of the mind, and most of all the power to detach one's own needs from the experience set forth in the poem. A moral sense so organized sets limits to human nature, and is content to observe them. But if the reader lack this moral sense, the poem will be only a body of abstractions either useful or irrelevant to that body of abstractions already forming, but of uncertain direction, in the reader's mind. This reader will see the poem chiefly as biography, and he will proceed to deduce from it a history of the poet's case, to which he will attach himself if his own case resembles it; if it doesn't, he will look for a more useful case. Either way, the poem as a specific object is ignored.

The reasoning that is being brought to bear upon Mr. Eliot's recent verse is as follows: Anglo-Catholicism would not at all satisfy me; therefore, his poetry declines under its influence. Moreover, the poetry is not "contemporary"; it doesn't solve any labor problems; it is special, personal; and it can do us no good. Now the poetry *is* special and personal in quality, which is one of its merits, but what the critics are really saying is this—that Eliot's case-history is not special at all, that it is a general scheme of possible conduct that will not do for them. To accept the poetry seems to amount to accepting an invitation to join the Anglican Church. For the assumption is that the poetry and the religious position are identical.

If this were so, why should not the excellence of the poetry induce writers to join the Church, in the hope of writing as well as Eliot, since the irrelevance of the Church to their own needs makes them reject the poetry? The answer is, of course, that both parts of this fallacy are common. There is an æsthetic Catholicism, and there is a communist-economic rejection of art because it is involved with the tabooed mode of salvation.

The belief is that Eliot's poetry—all other poetry—is a simple record of the responses of a personality to an environment. The belief witnesses the modern desire to judge an art scientifically, practically, industrially; according to how it works. The poetry is viewed first as a pragmatic instrument, then examined "critically" as a pragmatic result; neither stage of the approach gives us "useful" knowledge.

Now a different heredity-environment combination would give us, of mechanical necessity, a different result, a different quantity of power to do a different and perhaps better social work. Doubtless that is true. But there is something disconcerting in this simple solution to the problem when it is looked at more closely. Two vastly different records or case-histories might give us, qualitatively speaking, very similar results: Baudelaire and Eliot have in common many *qualities* but *no history*. Their "results" have at least the common features of irony, humility, introspection, reverence—qualities fit only for contemplation and not for judgment according to their utility in our own conduct.

It is in this, the qualitative sense, that Eliot's recent poetry has been misunderstood. In this sense, the poetry is special, personal, of no use, and highly distinguished. But it is held to be a general formula, not distinct from the general formula that Eliot repeated when he went into the Church.

The form of the poems in *Ash Wednesday* is lyrical and solitary, and there is almost none of the elaborate natural description and allusion that gave to *The Waste Land* a partly realistic and partly symbolic character. These six poems are a brief moment of religious experience in an age that believes religion to be a kind of defeatism and puts all its hope for man in finding the right secular order. The mixed realism and symbolism of *The Waste Land* issued in irony. The direct and lyrical method of the new poems is based upon the simpler quality of humility. The latter quality comes directly out of the former, and there is an even continuity in Eliot's work.

In *The Waste Land* the prestige of our secular faith gave to the style its special character. This faith was the hard, coherent medium through which the discredited forms of the historic cultures emerged only to be stifled; the poem is at once their vindication and the recognition of their defeat. They are defeated in fact, as a politician may be defeated by the popular vote, but their vindication consists in the critical irony that their subordinate position casts upon the modern world.

The typical scene is the seduction of the stenographer by the clerk, in *The Fire Sermon*. Perhaps Mr. J. W. Krutch has not discussed this scene, but a whole generation of critics has, and from a viewpoint that Mr. Krutch has recently made popular: the seduction betrays the disillusion of the poet. The mechanical, brutal scene shows what love really is—that is to say, what it is scientifically, since science is truth: it is only an act of practical necessity, for procreation. The telling of the story by the Greek seer, who is chosen from a past of illusion and ignorance, permits the scene to become *a satire on the unscientific values of the past.* It was all pretense to think that love was anything but a biological necessity. The values of the past were pretty, absurd, and false; the scientific truth is both true and bitter. This is the familiar romantic dilemma, and the critics have read it into the scene from their own romantic despair.

There is no despair in the scene itself. The critics, who being in the state of mind I have described are necessarily blind to an effect of irony, have mistaken the symbols of an ironic contrast for the terms of a philosophic dilemma. It is the kind of metaphorical "logic" typical of romantic criticism since Walter Pater. Mr. Eliot knows too much about classical irony to be overwhelmed by a popular dogma in literary biology. For the seduction scene shows, not what man is, but what *for a moment* he thinks he is. In other words, the clerk stands for the secularization of the religious and qualitative values in the modern world. And the meaning of the contrast between Tiresias and the clerk is not disillusion, but irony. The scene is a masterpiece, perhaps the more profound vision that we have of modern man.

The importance of this scene as a key to the intention of *Ash Wednesday* lies in the moral identity of humility and irony and in an important difference between them æsthetically. Humility is subjective, a quality of the moral character: it is thus general, invisible, and can only be inferred, not seen. *Irony is the visible, particular, and objective instance of humility.* Irony is the objective quality of an event or situation which stimulates our capacity for humility. It is that arrangement of experience, either premeditated by art or accidentally appearing in the affairs of men, which permits to the spectator an insight superior to that of the actor; it shows him that the practical program, the special ambition, of the actor at that moment is bound to fail. The humility thus derived is the self-respect proceeding from a sense of the folly of men in their desire to dominate a natural force or a situation. The seduction scene is the picture of modern and dominating man. The arrogance and the pride of conquest of the "small house agent's clerk" are the badge of science, bumptious practicality, overweening secular faith. The very success of his conquest witnesses its aimless character; it succeeds as a wheel succeeds in turning; he can only conquer again.

His own failure to understand his position is irony, and

the poet's insight into it is humility. But for the grace of
God, says the poet in effect, there go I. This is essentially
the poetic attitude, an attitude that Eliot has been approaching with increasing purity. It is not that his recent
verse is better than that of the period ending with *The
Waste Land*. Actually it is less spectacular and less complex in subject-matter; for Eliot less frequently objecti-
fies his leading emotion, humility, into irony. His new
form is simple, expressive, homogeneous, and direct, and
without the early elements of violent contrast.

There is a single ironic passage in *Ash Wednesday,* and
significantly enough it is the first stanza of the first poem.
This passage presents objectively the poet *as he thinks
himself for the moment to be*. It establishes that humility
towards his own merit which fixes the mode of the poems
that follow. And the irony has been overlooked by the
critics because they take the stanza as a literal exposition
of the latest phase of the Eliot *case-history*—at a time
when, in the words of Mr. Edmund Wilson, "his psychological plight seems most depressing." Thus, here is the
vain pose of a Titan too young to be weary of strife, but
weary of it nevertheless.

> Because I do not hope to turn again
> Because I do not hope
> Because I do not hope to turn
> Desiring this man's gift and that man's scope
> I no longer strive to strive towards such things
> (Why should the aged eagle stretch its wings?)
> Why should I mourn
> The vanished power of the usual reign?

If the six poems are taken together as the focus of a specific religious emotion, the opening stanza, instead of being a naïve personal "confession," appears in the less lurid light of a highly effective technical performance. This stanza has two features that are necessary to the development of the unique imagery which distinguishes the religious emotion of *Ash Wednesday* from any other religious poetry of our time. It is possibly the only kind of imagery that is valid for religious verse today.

The first feature is the regular yet halting rhythm, the smooth uncertainty of movement which may either proceed to greater regularity or fall away into improvisation. The second feature is the imagery itself. It is trite; it echoes two familiar passages from English poetry. But the quality to be observed is this: it is secular imagery. It sets forth a special ironic situation, but the emotion is not identified with any specific experience. The imagery is thus perfectly suited to the broken rhythm. The stanza is a device for getting the poem under way, starting from a known and general emotion, in a monotonous rhythm, for a direction which, to the reader, is unknown. The ease, the absence of surprise, with which Eliot proceeds to bring out the subject of his meditation is admirable. After some further and ironic deprecation of his worldly powers, he goes on:

> And pray to God to have mercy upon us
> And pray that I may forget
> These matters that with myself I too much discuss,
> Too much explain.

We are being told, of course, that there is to be some kind of discourse on God, or a meditation; yet the emotion is still general. The imagery is even flatter than before; it is "poetical" at all only in that special context; for it is the diction of prose. And yet, subtly and imperceptibly, the rhythm has changed; it is irregular and labored. We are being prepared for a new and sudden effect, and it comes in the first lines of the second poem:

Lady, three white leopards sat under a juniper-tree
In the cool of the day, having fed to satiety
On my legs my heart my liver and that which had been contained
In the hollow round of my skull. And God said
Shall these bones live? shall these
Bones live?

From here on, in all the poems, there is constant and sudden change of rhythm, and there is a corresponding alternation of two kinds of imagery—the visual and tactile imagery common to all poetry, without significance in itself for any kind of experience, and the traditional religious symbols. The two orders are inextricably fused.

It is evident that Eliot has hit upon the only method now available of using the conventional religious image in poetry. He has reduced it from symbol to image, from abstraction to the plane of sensation. And corresponding to this process, there are images of his own invention which he almost pushes over the boundary of sensation into abstractions, where they have the appearance of conventional symbols. The passage I have quoted above is an example of this: for the "Lady" may be a nun, or even the Virgin, or again she may be a beautiful woman; but she is presented, through the serious tone of the invocation, with all the solemnity of a religious figure. The fifth poem exhibits the reverse of the process; it begins with a series of plays on the Logos, the most rarefied of all the Christian abstractions; and it succeeds in creating the effect of immediate experience by means of a broken and distracted rhythm:

> If the lost word is lost, if the spent word is spent
> If the unheard, unspoken
> Word is unspoken, unheard;
> Still is the unspoken word, the word unheard,
> The word without a word, the Word within
> The world and for the world. . . .

1931

EDNA ST. VINCENT MILLAY*

MORE than any other living American poet, with the possible exception of T. S. Eliot, Miss Millay has puzzled her critics. Contrary to the conventional opinion, her poetry is no better understood than Eliot's, in spite of its greater simplicity, its more conventional meters, and its closer fulfillment of the popular notion of poetic language. Her particular kind of excellence is beyond much dispute, but it is difficult to appraise. She is the most written about of living poets, but her critics are partisans. They like her too well or not enough. These views are unfair; what is worse, they are misleading. Less interested readers of Miss Millay are tired of violent opinion. The more sceptical, embarrassed by her popularity in an age of uncertain and eclectic taste, do not take the trouble to find in her what is good.

This, too, is misleading and unfair. Apart from her merit as a poet, Miss Millay has been, not at all to her discredit, the spokesman of a generation. We do not need to enquire how she came to express the emotions of the literary generation that seized the popular imagination from about 1917 to 1925. It is a fact that she did, and in such a way as to remain the most typical poet of that generation. Her diverting mixture of solemnity and levity

* *Fatal Interview.* By Edna St. Vincent Millay. New York, 1931.

won the enthusiasm of a time intellectually bewildered but moving unsteadily towards an "emotional attitude"— as the phrase went in those days.

It was the age of the *Seven Arts,* of the old *Masses,* of the Provincetown Theatre, of the figure and disciples of Randolph Bourne. It has been called the age of experiment and liberation. There is still experiment, but there is no liberation. And that age is now dead.

Miss Millay helped to form her generation, and was formed by it. But she has survived her own time. Her statement about those times, in *A Few Figs from Thistles* and *Second April,* was not profound; morally, it has been said, it did perceptible damage to our young American womanhood, whose virgin impatience competed noisily with the Armistice and the industrial boom. There were suicides after *Werther* and seductions after *Don Juan.* Neither Byron nor Miss Millay is of the first order of poets. They are distinguished examples of the second order, without which literature could not bear the weight of Dante and Shakespeare, and without which poetry would lose its average sensibility, and become too specialized.

Being this kind of poet, Miss Millay was not prepared to clear up the point of view of her generation: her poetry does not define the break with the nineteenth century. This task was left to the school of Eliot, and it was predictable that Eliot should be—except by young men who had the experience to share Eliot's problem—ignored and misunderstood. Eliot penetrated to the fundamental structure of the nineteenth-century mind and showed its break-down. Miss Millay assumed no such profound alteration of the intelligence because, I suppose, not being an intellect but a sensibility, she was not aware of it. She foreshadowed an age without bringing it to terms. Taking the vocabulary of nineteenth-century poetry as pure as you will find it in Christina Rossetti, and drawing upon the stock of conventional imagery accumulated from Drayton to Housman, she has created, out of shopworn materials, an interesting personal attitude: she has been able to use the language of the preceding generation to convey an emotion peculiar to her own.

The decadent generation—Moody, Woodberry, and Louise Imogene Guiney—had more than Miss Millay has; but she has all that they had which was not dead. By making their language personal she has fought it back to life. This is her distinction. It is also her limitation. As a limitation it is not peculiar to her, her age or any age, but common to all ages; it is the quality that defines Collins and Gray, and poets like the Rossettis and Tennyson. Poets of this second order lack the power of creation in the proper sense in which something like a complete world is achieved, either in the vast, systematic vision of Milton, or in the allusive power of Webster and Shakespeare: backed only by a piece of common action, an entire world is set up in a line or even in a single phrase. In these poets the imaginative focus is less on the personal emotion than on its sub-structure, an order of spiritual life, and thus their very symbolism acquires not only a heightened significance but an independent existence of its own.

Not so with Miss Millay; we feel that she never penetrates to the depth of her symbols, but uses them chiefly as an external frame of reference, an adornment to the tale. It has been frequently and quite justly remarked that Miss Millay uses her classical symbols better than any other living poet; we should add, I believe, that she uses them conventionally better. She takes them literally, subtracting from them only what serves her metaphor; whereas an even more "modern" poet like Yeats is capable, in his sonnet *Leda,* of that violent addition to the content of the symbol as he finds it, which is the mark of great poetry.

Miss Millay's success with stock symbolism is precariously won. I have said that she is not an intellect but a sensibility: if she were capable of a profound analysis of her imagery she might not use it: such an analysis might disaffect her with the style that she so easily assumed, without necessarily leading her, as Yeats was led in mid-career, to create a new style of her own. The beautiful final sonnet of the sequence is a perfect specimen of her talent, and it is probably the finest poem she has written

> Oh, sleep forever in the Latmian cave,
> Mortal Endymion, darling of the moon!
> Her silver garments by the senseless wave
> Shouldered and dropped and on the shingle strewn,
> Her fluttering hand against her forehead pressed,
> Her scattered looks that trouble all the sky,
> Her rapid footsteps running down the west—

Of all her altered state, oblivious lie!
Whom earthen you, by deathless lips adored,
Wild-eyed and stammering to the grasses thrust,
And deep into her crystal body poured
The hot and sorrowful sweetness of the dust:
Whereof she wanders mad, being all unfit
For mortal love, that might not die of it.

We have only to compare this, good as it is, with Mr. Yeats' *Leda* to see the difference between the two kinds of symbol that I have described. The difference is first of all one of concentration and intensity; and finally a difference between an accurate picture of an emotion and an act of the imagination:

A sudden blow: the great wings beating still
Above the staggering girl, her thighs caressed
By the dark webs, her nape caught in his bill,
He holds her helpless breast upon his breast.
How can those terrified vague fingers push
The feathered glory from her loosening thighs?
And how can body, laid in that white rush
But feel the strange heart beating where it lies?
A shudder in the loins engenders there
The broken wall, the burning roof and tower
And Agamemnon dead.
                    Being so caught up,
So mastered by the brute blood of the air,
Did she put on his knowledge with his power
Before the indifferent beak could let her drop?

In an age which, in Mr. Pound's phrase, has "demanded an image"; in an age which has searched for a new construction of the mind, and has, in effect, asked every poet for a chart of salvation, it has been forgotten that one of the most valuable kinds of poetry may be deficient in imagination, and yet be valuable for the manner in which it meets its own defect. Miss Millay not only has given us the personality of her age; she has preserved it in the easiest traditional style. But there are those who will have no minor poets; these readers Miss Millay does not please. The others, her not too enthusiastic but perhaps misguided partisans, have seen too much of their own personalities in her verse to care whether it is great poetry or not; so they proceed to call it great.

It is doubtful if all of Miss Millay's previous work put together is worth the thin volume of these fifty-two sonnets. At no previous time has she given us so sustained a performance. Half of the sonnets, perhaps all but about fifteen, lack distinction. None is deficient in an almost final technique. From first to last every sonnet has its special rhythm and sharply-defined imagery. They move like a smooth machine, but not machine-like, under the hand of an expert technician. The best sonnets would adorn any of the great English sequences.

The serious, austere tone of her later work must not deceive us: she is the poet of ten years ago. She has been from the beginning the one poet of our time who has successfully stood athwart two ages; she has put the personality of her age into the style of the preceding age, without altering either. Of her it may be said, as of the late Elinor Wylie, that properly speaking she has no style, but has subtly transformed to her use the indefinable average of poetic English. We have seen the limitations of this order of talent. When the personal impulse weakens in a mind that cannot re-create a symbol and invent a style, we get the pastiche of *The Buck in the Snow:* the defects of such a talent are defects of taste, while the defects of Blake or Donne are mere blunders. Let us say no more of it. Miss Millay is one of our most valuable poets. But we should do well to misunderstand her as little as possible.

1931

E. E. CUMMINGS

THE quality of *Viva,** being quite uniform with that of Mr. Cummings' previous books, imposes upon the reviewer no obligation to describe important changes, in this poet's work, of style, composition, or point of view. This fact alone is, of course, of no significance, but it brings to the reviewer a grateful feeling of relief; it permits him to write with a full sense of the merit of the three previous books of verse by this poet, a sense that corrects, as it should, a feeling of disappointment in the quality of *Viva.*

It is not that the quality has fallen off. Cummings' faults are well-known, I believe, if not generally defined, and they are still essentially the faults of *Tulips and Chimneys* (1923). In that book it was not easy to distinguish his own quality, and thus his limitations, from the influence of other poets, Keats and Swinburne; but this influence has disappeared. The special quality of his talent stands forth without the misleading features of an unformed style. He has refined his talent, perhaps not to the point of which it is ideally capable, but at least to the

---

* Viva (seventy new poems). By E. E. Cummings. Horace Liveright, Inc., 1931.

point at which he is able to convey a particular kind of meaning that very properly obsesses any poet in contact with his medium.

His uniformity is not uniformity of style. The point could be labored, but I think it is sufficient to refer the reader of Cummings to the three distinct styles of poems XVIII, LI, and LVII in *Viva*. He has a great many styles, and having these he has none at all—a feature of his poetry concealed by his famous device of distorted word and line. For style is that quality of a piece of writing which may be distinguished from its communicable content but which in no sense can be subtracted from it: the typographical device can be so subtracted by simple alteration either in the direction of conventional pattern or in the direction of greater distortion. The typography is distinct from style, something superimposed and external to the poem, a mechanical system of variety and a formula of surprise; it is—and this is its function—a pseudo-dynamic feature that galvanizes the imagery with the look of movement, of freedom or fresh perception, a kind of stylization which is a substitute for a living relation between the images and the sensibility of the poet. Mr. Cummings' imagery reaches the page still-born.

This characteristic of his verse has been brilliantly analyzed by Mr. R. P. Blackmur, in his *Notes on E. E. Cummings' Language.** To that essay I refer the reader for a discussion of Cummings' replacement of stock

---

* *The Double Agent: Essays in Craft and Elucidation.* By R. P. Blackmur. New York: Arrow Editions, 1935.

poetic conventions with an equally limited set of conventions of his own. "By denying the dead intelligence and putting on the heresy of unintelligence," says Mr. Blackmur, "the poet only succeeds in substituting one set of unnourished conventions for another." Again: "As if sensation could be anything more than the idea of sensation . . . without being attached to some central body of experience, genuinely understood and *formed* in the mind." And Mr. Blackmur summarizes his view: "So long as he is content to remain in his private mind, he is unknowable, impenetrable, and sentimental."

These statements reach to the center of Cummings' problem, but I believe that Mr. Blackmur takes too seriously the "heresy of unintelligence"; it is rather the heresy of supposing that personality, as such, outside the terms of something that is not personality, can ever be made known.

Now in addition to the typographical mechanism there is another that grows out of it—the mechanism of emotionally private words that are constantly overcharged into pseudo-symbols. This has two aspects. There is the repetition of single words (Mr. Blackmur, in his comprehensive study, examines in detail the personal *cliches:* "flower," "petal," "bloom," etc.); and there is the headlong series of miscellaneous words that attempt to imitate the simultaneity and shock of fresh sensation. Mr. Blackmur shows that the weight of the series cancels the sensory value of its single items. Both this device and the distorted line probably proceed from the poet's sense of the insufficiency of his style: there is something wrong, something obscure that demands a superimposed heightening for effect.

Without this external variety we get, in Cummings, the uniformity that I have mentioned, but it is rather a uniformity of meaning, of reference, than of conception. No single poem introduces the reader to an implicit body of idea beneath its surface, a realm of meaning detached once and for all from the poet. We go on to the next poem, and from the aggregate of Mr. Cummings' poems we return to the image of his personality: like all poets he seems to say "more" than the explicit terms convey, but this "more" lies in the origin of the poem, not in the tension of its materials. From *To His Coy Mistress* we derive no clue to the existence of such a person as "Andrew Marvel"; from *Viva* we get only the evidence of personality. And this is what Cummings' poetry "means." It is a kind of meaning very common at present; Cummings is the original head of an easily imitable school. This does not mean that he has ever been successfully imitated; no one else of his generation has written personal poetry as well as Mr. Cummings writes it. It is rather that he has shown the possibility of making personal conventions whose origin and limit are personality. It is a kind of convention that, given "talent," can make of any one a poet. It requires a certain interest in oneself, which permits one to ascribe to one's "feeling-tone" for words an objective meaning, a comprehensible meaning to the relations existing among those words. This stanza,

by no means an extreme example of pure "feeling-tone,"
illustrates the process:

> your slightest look easily will unclose me
> though I have closed myself as fingers,
> you open always petal by petal myself as Spring opens
> (touching skillfully, mysteriously) her first rose

There is sententiousness in excess of an occasion that remains "unknowable," and we are brought back to the
poet who becomes the conceivable reference of an emotion in excess of what is said. But "Cummings" in that
sense is an empty abstraction, and the fact that the poet
Cummings leads us there, away from the poem itself,
explains Mr. Blackmur's remark that the poetry exists
only in terms of something that is "impenetrable" and
"sentimental." It fails to implicate the reader with the
terms of a *formed* body of experience. The poet asks us
at last not to attend to the poem as poetry, but to its interesting origin, the poet who, the publisher assures us,
has a "cheerful disdain for the approval of pundits and
poetasters."

In Mr. Cummings' work there is much that amuses
and much that one admires. A rigorous selection from his
four books would give us some of the best poetry of the
age. In *&,* the magnificent sonnet on death, and the love
sonnet ending "an inch of nothing for your soul," though
projected in Mr. Cummings' personal imagery, achieve
a measure of objective validity by reference to the traditional imagery of such poetry, which he inverts, but by

implication leans upon. His best verse is that in which he succeeds, perhaps unintentionally, in escaping from his own personality into a world of meaning that not even the "heresy of unintelligence" can let him ignore. For this reason he cannot forever be immune to the heavy hand of the pundits. If he finds their pretensions tiresome, he will agree with me that it is the fate of interesting personalities to be continually bored.

1932

INDEX

INDEX

237

INDEX

Davies, Sir John, 74, 76
Decline of the West, The, 94 n.
Democracy and Leadership, 121
Demon of the Absolute, The, 133
Denham, Sir John, 211
Dewey, John, 35
Dialogues, Plato's, 128
Dickinson, Emily, 3–24, 111, 148
Divine Comedy, The, 33, 89, 92
Divine Poems, 68
Donne, John, 3, 12, 17, 20, 64–73, 81, 227
Double Agent, The, 229 n.
Drayton, Michael, 73, 223
Dryden, John, 65, 72, 93
Dunbar, William, 81

Eastman, Max, 146
Edwards, Jonathan, 10
Elegies, Donne's, 68
Eliot, "Apostle," 6
Eliot, T. S., 26, 31, 52, 57, 65, 69, 81, 127, 136, 171, 200, 204–206, 210 ff., 221, 222
Extasie, The, 67

Faërie Queene, The, 82, 90
Fatal Interview, 221 ff.; sonnet LII quoted, 224
Fernandez, Ramon, 143
Few Figs from Thistles, A, 222
Fitts, Dudley, 202
Foerster, Norman, 113–144
Ford, John, 78
Form, related to language, 53–63; related to symbol, 26–41, 62; related to metrics, 54–55; plastic, 62
For the Marriage of Faustus and Helen, 30–31
Frick, Henry Clay, 123

Garland for John Donne, A, 64 ff., 77 n.
Gascoigne, David, 74
Gautier, Théophile, 62
Glasgow, Ellen, 164
Glory of the Nightingales, The, 196
Golden Age, The, 97–99
Golden Ass, The, 50
"Go, Soul, the body's guest," 77
Gower, John, 78
Gray, Thomas, 223
Greek Tradition, The, 129

Greene, Robert, 79
Gregory, Horace, 52
Greville, Fulke, 75–76
Grimald, Nicholas, 71
Guiney, Louise Imogene, 223

Hall, John, 76
Hardy, Thomas, 24, 201
Hawthorne, Nathaniel, 6, 8, 10–12, 24, 91, 148
Hayward, John, 65
Hegel, G. W. F., 173
Herbert, George, 17
Hérédia, de, José-Maria, 62
Hicks, Granville, 53
Higginson, T. W., 21, 24
Hind and the Panther, The, 93
Holmes, Oliver Wendell, 7
Housman, A. E., 223
Hulme, T. E., 49, 170
Humanism, 113–144
Huxley, T. H., 16
Hyperion, 42, 146

Imagism, 68
Induction to the Mirror for Magistrates, 75, 77, 79
In Memoriam, 69
Intellectualism, in poetry, 21; in religion, 130
Irony, Romantic, 83, 87, 96–97, 102, 105, 108, 215–217; classical, 37, 215

James, Henry, 11, 12, 185
Jeffers, Robinson, 70, 103
Jefferson, Thomas, 151, 184, 188
Jew of Malta, The, 78
John Brown's Body, 89
Johnson, Samuel, 64, 159, 211

Keats, John, 42, 228
Kepler, Johann, 66
King Lear, 85
Knox, John, 150
Krutch, Joseph Wood, 215

Lachrymæ Christi, 40
Lancelot, 195
Landor, Walter Savage, 80, 111
Laud, Archbishop, 5
Leda, 224; quoted, 225
Longfellow, H. W., 7, 23

238

INDEX

INDEX

Shakespeare, William, 20, 21, 24, 82, 83, 87, 111, 143, 166, 222, 223
Shelley, P. B., 20, 84-86, 96-97, 103, 208
Shepherd's Calendar, The, 54, 75
Sidney, Sir Philip, 53, 77-79
Simms, William Gilmore, 148
Simpson, Evelyn M., 65, 77 n.
Slavery, Effect of, on Southern culture, 154 ff.
Smith, Adam, 182
Songs and Sonets, Donne's, 68
Songs and Sonets, Tottel's, 75
Sophocles, 124-125
Sorrows of Werther, The, 222
Sparrow, John, 65
Spencer, Theodore, 64 ff.
Spender, Stephen, 103 n.
Spengler, Oswald, 94 n.
Spenser, Edmund, 53, 75, 77-80, 82
Stein, Leo, 109
Studies of Religious Dualism, 129 ff.
Summa Theologiæ, 124
Surrey, Henry Howard, Earl of, 71
Swinburne, A. C., 228

Taggard, Genevieve, 8
Taine, H.-A., 95
Talifer, 195 ff.
Tempest, The, 98
Tennyson, Alfred, 16, 20, 69, 99, 223
Theocracy, 4 ff.
Thucydides, 187
To His Coy Mistress, 231
To His Lute, 84
Torrent and the Night Before, The, 193
Tourneur, Cyril, 76
Town Down the River, The, 193

Tradition, in poetry, 17 ff.; and authority, 113 ff., 135; and religion, 125 ff., 175 ff.
Trent, William Peterfield, 154
Tristram, 195, 198
Tulips and Chimneys, 228
Tunnel, The, 37

Valediction Forbidding Mourning, A, 67
Van Doren, Mark, 193-194, 198
Vaughan, Henry, 17
Vergil, 124-125
Verlaine, Paul, 145
Villon, François, 22, 138
Viva, 228 ff.
Voltaire, de, François Marie Arouet, 161

Waller, Edmund, 208
Warren, Robert Penn, 7
Waste Land, The, 107, 171, 214-217
Webster, John, 78, 223
Wells, H. G., 147
Wesley, John, 150
Whipple, T. K., 77 n.
White Buildings, 28, 30-31
Whitman, Walt, 24, 32
Williamson, George, 69
Wilson, Edmund, 55, 81, 100, 105, 217
Woodberry, George Edward, 223
Wordsworth, William, 86
Wyat, Sir Thomas, 71, 74-75, 79, 208
Wylie, Elinor, 69, 226

Yeats, William Butler, 56-57, 81, 87, 224; *Leda* quoted, 225
Young, Stark, 164